TWAYNE'S WORLD LEADERS SERIES

EDITOR OF THIS VOLUME

Arthur W. Brown
*Baruch College, The City University
of New York*

Woodrow Wilson

TWLS 76

Woodrow Wilson

WOODROW WILSON

By DAVID D. ANDERSON
Michigan State University

TWAYNE PUBLISHERS
A DIVISION OF G. K. HALL & CO., BOSTON

Published in 1978 by Twayne Publishers,
A Division of G. K. Hall & Co.
All Rights Reserved

Printed on permanent/durable acid-free paper and bound
in the United States of America

First Printing

Library of Congress Cataloging in Publication Data

Anderson, David D
Woodrow Wilson.

(Twayne's world leaders series ; TWLS 76)
Bibliography: p. 160-63
Includes index.
1. Wilson, Woodrow, Pres. U.S., 1856-1924.
2. Presidents—United States—Biography.
E767.A53   973.91'3'0924 [B]   78-17169
ISBN 0-8057-7705-9

To the memory of my father,
David J. Anderson
1898–1973

Contents

About the Author

David D. Anderson's long interest in American literary and intellectual history and criticism has produced sixteen books, including four for Twayne, *Louis Bromfield* (TUSAS), *Brand Whitlock* (TUSAS), *Abraham Lincoln* (TUSAS), and *Robert Ingersoll* (TUSAS), and hundreds of articles, essays, and short stories in the *Yale Review, Mark Twain Journal,* the *Personalist,* and many other journals. He is currently editor of the *University College Quarterly* and *MidAmerica,* the yearbook of the Society for the Study of Midwestern Literature, which he founded in 1971.

Recipient of many awards, including the Distinguished Faculty Award from Michigan State University, where he is Professor of American Thought and Language, and the Distinguished Alumnus Award from Bowling Green State University, he was Fulbright Professor of American Literature at the University of Karachi, Pakistan, and he has lectured throughout Europe, Asia, and Australia. He is currently at work on *William Jennings Bryan* for Twayne, a photo biography of Sherwood Anderson, and a cultural history of the Midwest.

Preface

Of the thirty-nine men who have occupied the office of the Presidency, Thomas Woodrow Wilson was perhaps the most complex. Teacher, scholar, academic administrator, governor, President, world leader, he was in each of these dimensions of a varied career simultaneously a practical man and a philosopher. And as both practical man and philosopher he was a forceful, gifted, often eloquent writer, the master of a prose style that brought life and color to such varied but usually prosaic documents as college textbooks and state papers.

The complexity of the man is clearly demonstrated in the breadth and depth of his public life and the major place in American and world history that he continues to occupy; nowhere, however, is Wilson's complexity more evident than in responses by those who knew him to the relationship between his personality and his Presidency. Almost invariably those reactions find their expressions in oversimplifications as varied as William Allen White's four-line editorial obituary and the elaborate psychoanalysis by Sigmund Freud, who did not know Wilson, in collaboration with William C. Bullitt, who did. For White, the complexity could most easily be expressed in the traditional dichotomy of good and evil:

> God gave him a great vision.
> The Devil gave him an imperious heart.
> The proud heart is still.
> The vision lives.

However, for Bullitt, who in 1920 persuaded Freud to collaborate with him in an elaborate psychoanalysis of a man whom Freud had never known, to be published after the deaths of the subject and his wife, Wilson's complexity could best be defined in the argot of Freudian psychology. The result is a conclusion no less oversimplified in spite of its profundity than that of William Allen White: the psychological foundation of Wilson's complexity, according to the founder of modern psychoanalysis and to a diplomat trusted by Wilson, was a curious love-hate relationship with his father, a relationship that contributed to the imperiousness of Wilson's nature and ultimately affected, for better or worse, the history of civilization.

To their credit, both the four-line obituary and the exhaustive psychoanalysis seek explanations in terms that reflect universal human experience as well as the particulars of Wilson's often-quoted remark made in a sentimental moment that "A boy never gets over his boyhood." Nevertheless, too often the combination of a Southern post–Civil War background and an indoctrination in the principles of John Calvin, fuel for the environmentalists, the psychoanalysts, and the moralists, is seen as the key to Wilson's public roles as scholar, as president of Princeton, as President of the United States, and as maker of war and seeker of peace.

These interpretations are as appealing as they are ultimately unsatisfactory because they, in common with White, with Bullitt and Freud, and with the authors of the many historical studies who have seen Wilson in his varied roles as an actor in a particularly dramatic period of American history, ignore a vital fact in the Wilson record: the remarkable intellectual growth revealed by the written record of Wilson's voluminous writings. Wilson was and remained a moralist; he was and remained a critic of government in the abstract and of specific governments and governmental functions; he demanded a high standard of performance from himself and from those who worked with and for him; many of his consistencies as well as his inconsistencies are difficult to explain except in terms dominated by abstractions rather than commonplaces of human experience.

All this is evident in Wilson's own words, written throughout the course of a long career that, in spite of its apparent diversity, was marked by a curiously progressive consistency. From a middle-class Georgia parsonage to the White House, growth, change, and consistency run in parallel patterns in Wilson's writings, and in the course of those patterns it becomes evident that Wilson's moralism began in narrow sectarianism but ultimately took on universal dimensions; his concept of the ideal government was rooted in rational British parliamentarianism but eventually found its expression in a search for human brotherhood almost mystic in nature; his demand for a high standard of human performance began in an emphasis upon trivialities but found its culmination in a willingness to make the ultimate sacrifice for the greatest human good; his often inexplicable predictability and equally often inexplicable unpredictability merge in a curiously progressive pattern through a life that ranged from a petulant search for some of the many levels of personal power to an enfranchisement of all mankind.

All this is evident in a personal record that is not only more complete but more eloquent than that of any other President. While Lincoln at times rose to higher levels of expression and later Presidents, from Franklin D. Roosevelt to Richard Nixon, have compiled greater masses of paper, Wilson's record is uniquely his own because it is characterized from beginning to end by his high regard for language, his determination to express himself clearly and forcefully as well as eloquently, and, even in the most demanding moments of his Presidency, his conviction that no ghost writer, no assistant, no secretary, no committee, could or should substitute for his own words or come between him and his listeners and his readers.

Before Wilson was President, he was a man of letters, as were several of his predecessors, although, oddly, none of his successors; but unlike those who came before him as well as after him, even in the Presidency he remained a man of letters; his high regard for language itself, his search for clarity and aesthetic stimulation in the spoken and written word, and his awareness of the power of language as a motivating means to ends petty or noble remained with him to the end.

In spite of the fascination with which generations of scholars, journalists, public figures, and others have approached Wilson in hundreds of articles, essays, memoirs, and books, this record, that of Woodrow Wilson as a writer, remains largely unwritten until now, and it is this record that I hope to define as completely as can be done within the limitations imposed by the dimensions of this volume. In attempting this definition my focus will remain on Wilson's literary legacy to America, a record that ranges from the five-volume *A History of the American People* to individual letters and memoranda.

Futhermore, Woodrow Wilson was one of the most controversial of Presidents in his own time, and to a degree he remains so today among historians, social commentators, and those interested in the continued unfolding of the American epic. Attempts at interpretation are as numerous as the possible interpretations of the significance of his personality and his Presidency, but I do not attempt to enter the former controversy, except in certain obvious misstatements of fact, and in the case of William Bayard Hale's vicious attack on Wilson as a prose stylist in his 1920 publication *The Story of a Style*, which has unfortunately become the basis of too many general statements about the aesthetic qualities of his writing. In spite of my sympathy for Wilson, I hope that my assessment of him as a writer and a President will remain unbiased.

Because most of Wilson's conscious literary effort was expended before he entered public life, the form of this study will differ from most more conventional studies of Wilson, which give comparatively little attention to the writing of his academic career and much more to that of his Presidency. However, my emphasis upon Wilson's writing and the development of his style and thinking requires a much larger than usual emphasis upon those early years, and much of my assessment of Wilson as a writer is based upon them.

In making that assessment I am not attempting to write biography, social or political history, or personality analysis or appraisal; I am attempting to define the nature of Wilson's accomplishments as a writer and the course of his development as a thinker. Biography, social and political history, perhaps something of the sweep of the times, will appear in these pages, but only as they illuminate what Wilson has written.

The documentary record of Wilson's contemporaries and particularly his intimates is as complete as his own, and I plan to draw on these records as well when they illuminate Wilson's own works. The tools of modern literary criticism are as varied as the works upon which they are employed, and I propose to use those which enable me to approach a definition of the literary accomplishment of this complex, elusive, controversial man whose place in the history of man's search for fulfillment cannot be denied.

DAVID D. ANDERSON

Lansing, Michigan

Acknowledgments

For the many kinds of assistance that enabled me to write this book, I am deeply grateful: to the unfailingly helpful staffs of the Michigan State University Library, the State Library of Michigan, and the Lansing Public Library; to Mrs. Paul Rittenhour, Lawrence Ziewacz, and Pauline and Walter Adams for generously making books available; to friends and colleagues—Bernard Engel, Russel B. Nye, William McCann, William Thomas, Ben Strandness—for insights, stimulation, and comments; and, as always, to my wife Pat for her encouragement, interest, and assistance.

For another kind of help, less tangible but no less real, I am grateful to my father, the late David J. Anderson, to whom this book is inscribed. Not only did he serve in Mr. Wilson's war, but he shared his faith in Mr. Wilson with me.

Chapter 11, "Woodrow Wilson, Man of Letters," appeared in somewhat different form in *University College Quarterly*.

Chronology

1856   Woodrow Wilson born December 28 at Staunton, Virginia, the third child of the Reverend Joseph Ruggles Wilson and Janet Woodrow Wilson. Christened Thomas Woodrow Wilson.

1867– Attends Mr. Derry's Classical School in Augusta, Georgia.
1870

1870– Privately tutored in Latin and Greek by Mrs. Joseph R.
1874   Russell in Columbia, South Carolina.

1873– Attends Davidson College in North Carolina.
1874

1875– Attends Princeton University; edits *Princetonian;* sings in
1879   Glee Club; debates; graduates with B.A., June 1879.

1877   Publishes first article, "Prince Bismarck," in *Nassau Literary Magazine,* November 1877.

1878   Publishes prize essay, "William, Earl of Chatham," in *Nassau Literary Magazine,* October 1878.

1879   Publishes article, "Cabinet Government in the United States," in *International Review,* August 1879.

1879– Attends law school, University of Virginia. Leaves in De-
1880   cember because of poor health.

1880   Speaks on negative side of debate: "Is the Roman Catholic Element in the United States a Menace to American Institutions?" Text published in the *University of Virginia Magazine,* April 1880; publishes article signed "Atticus," "Mr. Gladstone—A Character Sketch," in *University of Virginia Magazine,* April 1880.

1881   Spends year at home regaining health.

1882   Admitted to the bar; practices in Atlanta, Georgia, with E. I. Rensick. Testifies before the Tariff Commission in September; leaves the practice of law in the fall.

1883– Studies for Ph.D. at Johns Hopkins University. Awarded
1885   Historial Fellowship.

1885   Publishes *Congressional Government;* marries Ellen Louise

Axson of Savannah, Georgia, on June 24; appointed Associate Professor of History and Political Economy, Bryn Mawr College, in September.

1886   Receives degree of Ph.D. from Johns Hopkins University.

1888– Occupies Chair of History and Political Economy, Wesleyan
1890   University.

1888   Lectures throughout New England and at Johns Hopkins.

1889   Publishes *The State: Elements of Historial and Practical Politics.*

1890– Occupies Chair of Jurisprudence and Politics at Princeton
1902   University.

1893   Publishes "Mr. Cleveland's Cabinet" in *Review of Reviews,* April; *An Old Master and Other Political Essays; Division and Reunion.*

1896   *Mere Literature and Other Essays; George Washington.*

1897   "Mr. Cleveland's Cabinet" and "The Making of the Nation" in *The Atlantic Monthly.*

1901   *When a Man Comes to Himself.*

1902   *A History of the American People* (5 vols.); elected president of Princeton University, July 3; inaugurated October 25.

1902– Serves as president of Princeton University.
1910

1903   "States' Rights" in *Cambridge Modern History.*

1904   Publishes a statement on the tutorial system in the *Princeton Alumni Weekly.*

1905   Publishes a statement on the Princeton preceptorial system in the *Independent,* August.

1906   Publishes notes on Constitutional Government.

1907   "Politics from 1857 to 1907" in *Atlantic Montly,* November.

1908   "The States and the Federal Government" in *North American Review,* May; *Constitutional Government in the United States.*

1909   "The Tariff Make-Believe" in *North American Review,* October; "What Is a College For?", *Scribner's Magazine,* November.

1910   "Living Principles of Democracy," *Harper's Weekly,* April 9; nominated Democratic candidate for governor of New Jersey, September; Resigns as president of Princeton University, October; elected governor of New Jersey by a majority of 49,000, November.

1911   Inaugural address as governor of New Jersey, January 17.

1912   First annual message to legislature of New Jersey, January 9; sends sixteen veto messages to senate of New Jersey, April 2; nominated as Democratic candidate for President of the United States, July 2; elected President of the United States, November 4.

1913–   Serves as twenty-seventh President of the United States.
1921

1913   *The New Freedom,* January; resigns as Governor of New Jersey, March 1; inaugurated President of the United States, March 4; issues statement on Mexican policy and revolutionary intrigue, March 11; requests revision of tariff, April 8; addresses joint session of Congress on currency legislation, June 23; delivers first annual address to Congress, December 2.

1914   Addresses joint session of Congress on trusts and monopolies, January 20; addresses joint session on Mexican policy, April 20; beginning of World War I, August 4; Mrs. Wilson dies, August 6; issues neutrality statement, August 19; delivers second annual address to joint session of Congress, December 8.

1915   Sends freedom of seas message to Germany, February 10; sends note to Germany on sinking of *Lusitania,* May 13; becomes engaged to Edith Bolling Galt, October 7; protests British blockade of neutral ports, October 21; delivers third annual address to joint houses of Congress, December 7; marries Edith Bolling Galt, December 18.

1916   Gives series of talks on national defense, January-February; presents memorandum on ending the war, February 22; renominated Democratic candidate for President, June 16; reelected President of the United States, November 7; delivers fourth annual address to joint session of Congress, December 5; sends peace message to belligerents, December 18.

1917   Addresses U.S. Senate on terms of peace in Europe, January 22; addresses joint session of Congress on German submarine policy, February 3; requests authority to arm merchant ships, February 26; issues statement to the country on "a little group of willful men," March 4; inaugurated President of the United States, March 5; requests declaration of war against Germany, April 2; delivers fifth annual address to joint session of Congress, December 4.

1918   Issues "Fourteen Points" at joint session of Congress, January 8; issues public statement on democracy, July 26; exchanges peace notes with Germany and Austria, October; announces armistice at joint session of Congress, November 11; delivers sixth annual message to joint session of Congress, December 2; sails for Europe, December 4, visits England.

1919   Speaks in Italy and France, January-February; opens Peace Conference, Paris, January 18; presents plan for League of Nations, February 14; returns to United States, February 24; returns to France, March 13; signs Treaty of Peace with Germany, June 28; returns to U.S., July 8; requests Senate approval of treaty, July 10; makes series of forty speeches in seventeen states in twenty-two days, September; taken ill, September 26; returns to Washington September 28; sends seventh annual message to two houses of Congress, December 2.

1920   Sends eighth annual message to the two houses of Congress, December 7; receives Nobel Peace Prize, December 10.

1921   Leaves office, March 4; moves to new home at 2340 S Street N.W., Washington, D.C.; rides in funeral procession for Unknown Soldier, November 11.

1922   Speaks to crowd before his home, January 15, and again on November 11.

1923   Participates in President Harding's funeral, August 8; publishes "The Road Away from Revolution" in *Atlantic Monthly*, August; speaks over radio on "The Significance of Armistice Day," November 10; addresses crowd at his home, November 11.

1924   Collapses, January 31; dies, February 3; buried in Bethlehem Chapel of the Washington Cathedral, February 6.

CHAPTER 1

The Formative Years

THE decade of the 1850s was not only the most critical but perhaps the most dramatic in American history. On the political level it began in the attempt at compromise as men of good will of diverse political and moral convictions sought to transcend the issue and meaning of slavery in order to prolong the life of the American republic. At the end of the decade secession and dissolution had become the American reality, and a chain of events had begun, the outcome of which no man could predict but which strong men from both sections were determined to direct in terms of their own convictions.

As dramatic as were the political events between the extremes of time and political fact—the struggles over definitions of liberty and democracy, over theoretical and practical interpretations of the relationships between units of government, the legal and extralegal attempts to come to terms with the dimensions of human freedom, the bloody battles over parts of the frontier American landscape, the passing of great leaders, the fragmentation of great political parties, and the emergence of a great leader whose destiny was to attempt to restore unity and extend freedom through the ultimate violence— other levels of American life were no less dramatic, if less spectacular or frightening.

Among these lesser but no less significant events were the transitions that saw Transcendentalists become Abolitionists, humanistic idealists become bloodthirsty warriors, constitutional jurists deny the validity of the law. The promise of the American experiment had, for many Americans, become a mockery of the ideals proclaimed as goals and statements of faith less than a century earlier. Liberty and union were abstractions almost universally subscribed to, but in practice they became qualified by the demands of partisan groups who asked such questions as: Liberty for whom? What are the conditions of union? Virtually no one of prominence was willing to subscribe publicly without qualification to a free federal union, although an obscure Illinois lawyer and former Congressman began increasingly to be heard as he insisted, like Daniel Webster before him, that liberty and union were absolute and inseparable. By the end of the decade, that obscure prairie laywer was President-elect of the United States, the sixteenth and, it appeared, perhaps the last President of the Republic.

Nevertheless, even while the Compromise of 1850 revealed itself as a compromise of principle rather than practicality, the Kansas-Nebraska controversy led to bloodshed, Dred Scott was denied his manhood, and John Brown found his martyrdom, the life of the Republic and of its people went on. The population in 1850 was 23 million; ten years later, it was 31 million; at the beginning of the decade, the course of empire had added California to the union, and only crisis had prevented the addition of other states; the decade saw such technological developments as linking New York and Chicago by rail, laying the Atlantic cable, and drilling the first oil well at Titusville, Pennsylvania.

I   *Ancestry*

On private, individual levels, the restless migration that had marked the course of American history continued as men moved West, South, and North, wherever fate and the promise of fulfillment led them. One of these was a young Presbyterian clergyman, Joseph Ruggles Wilson, who, having married at Chillicothe, Ohio, on June 7, 1849, had taken his young wife in succession to a brief pastorate in Pennsylvania; a professorship "extraordinary of rhetoric" at his alma mater, Jefferson College, also in Pennsylvania; a professorship of chemistry and the natural sciences at Hampden-Sidney College in Virginia; and, in 1855, the pastorate of the First Presbyterian Church at Staunton, Virginia. There, in the Presbyterian Manse, on December 28, 1856, his third child and the first of two sons, Thomas Woodrow Wilson, was born.[1]

Although Wilson and his critics were later to make much of his Virginia birth and Southern upbringing, both are of less significance in his development than his ancestry and his parentage. On both sides his ancestry was Scottish and Presbyterian. All of his grandparents were immigrants, as was his mother. His paternal grandparents, James Wilson and Anne Adams, arrived in Philadelphia in 1807, and, as James Wilson began his long association with the printing trade, they were married in 1808. Within a few years James Wilson became imbued with the political philosophy of Thomas Jefferson, and in 1812 he gained control of the *Aurora,* one of America's great early newspapers, and he became a spokesman for Jeffersonianism. But he felt the lure of the West and joined the migration across the mountains; in 1815 he became owner of the *Western Herald and Steubenville Gazette* of Steubenville, Ohio, another Democratic voice in ᴀ state just twelve years old, and he became active in Ohio politics, first as a member of the Ohio legislature and later as an associate judge of the Ohio Court of Common Pleas. Perhaps inevitably he came into conflict with the forces of Andrew Jackson as he supported the protective tariff and internal improvements, the cornerstones of Whiggery, and he declared for the independence of Congress and the supremacy of the federal union.

The father of seven sons, all of whom learned the printer's trade, and of three daughters, he was, at his death, a railroad incorporator, a real-estate speculator, and a bank director. His sudden death occurred in 1850 as he was building a fine house as a mark of his success and as a symbol of his role as a prominent citizen.

His oldest son, William, became a leading Pittsburgh publisher and later the editor of the *Chicago Tribune* and a leader of the Granger movement. He was the father of two Union army generals. His youngest son, Joseph Ruggles Wilson, father of Woodrow, was the family scholar, an increasingly prominent clergyman-educator, and, after his marriage to Jesse Woodrow of Chillicothe, Ohio, and his move South, a Southern sympathizer.

Jesse Woodrow was the daughter of the Reverend Dr. Thomas Woodrow, who had brought his family to American from Scotland, in 1836, accepting pastorates first in Canada and then in Chillicothe, where Jesse grew up, before moving on to the Hogg Presbyterian Church of Columbus, Ohio, where he remained until his death in 1877. The Woodrows were a large family and as poor as ministers' families have traditionally been, but they were conscious of a proud heritage and an ancestry not only studded with scholars and clergymen of prominence, but also with real or imagined connections with some of Scotland's great families, including the Bruces. The family sought education with a passion, and Jesse's brother, Dr. James Woodrow, became a prominent scientist and a proponent of the doctrine of evolution who, tried and found not guilty of propagating heresy by his presbytery, was nevertheless fired from his teaching position in the Columbia Theological Seminary in South Carolina. A veteran of the Confederate army medical department, he later became president of South Carolina College and a favorite of his sister's oldest son, Thomas Woodrow Wilson. James Woodrow never questioned either scientific or religious truth because, as he insisted, "God's work and God's plan cannot contradict each other."[2] In his trial he was supported not only by his father, but by his nephew, Thomas Woodrow Wilson, then a twenty-eight-year-old graduate student at Johns Hopkins.

Although in his undergraduate fancies at Princeton Woodrow Wilson often thought of himself as "Thomas Woodrow Wilson, [future] Senator from Virginia," Wilson's association with the state of his birth was brief. Before he was a year old, the family moved to Augusta, Georgia, where Joseph Wilson became pastor of the First Presbyterian Church. In Augusta Woodrow Wilson's memory began, and there he spent his formative years. Significant among both were the experiences of a small boy in the South during the Civil War. In later years he recalled someone say that because Abe Lincoln had been elected, there would be war. He remembered, too, that he had once seen General Lee, that he had seen federal troops take Jefferson Davis past him on his way to imprisonment in Fortress Monroe, and he remembered Union troops occupying his father's church while the streets of Augusta were full of bitter ex-Confederate soldiers and bewildered former slaves. But he remembered no suffering.

Of much importance was the devotion with which Woodrow Wilson's father supported the Southern cause, even at the cost of strained relations with his father and family in Ohio. James Wilson had long strongly opposed slavery in his papers, and as part of his break with the Jacksonians he supported a high protective tariff and accepted the new Republican political faith; his outlook was very nearly radical. Conversely, the Reverend Dr. Joseph Wilson was not only a political secessionist, but a religious one as well. The first general assembly of the Presbyterian Church of the South was held in his church, and from 1865 until 1898 he was Stated Clerk of the General Assembly of the Presbyterian church in the United States, the official title of the Southern branch.

However, during the war and the reconstruction that followed, Wilson's experiences centered upon a home life that was secure and apparently reasonably happy. His father's salary was adequate, and, as Sigmund Freud and William C. Bullitt have stressed so heavily, his relationship with his father was quite close. His father, former "Professor Extraordinary of Rhetoric," took charge of his education, the result of which was the fact that Woodrow Wilson's lifelong love affair with the English language, his lifelong loyalty to the Democratic party, and perhaps even his relatively late conversion to progressivism can be traced to his father's influence.

II *Education*

Joseph Wilson based his son's education upon the great nineteenth-century English writers, particularly Charles Dickens and Charles Lamb, but his love of oratory led him also to introduce his son to great American orators, even, interestingly enough, the late Daniel Webster. The focal point of Joseph Wilson's educational philosophy rested upon the language itself and the precision, clarity, and eloquence with which the individual words, phrases, and sentences might ideally transmit ideas. Father and son practiced rewriting Lamb and Webster, while reading Dickens and Scott together.

His father's lessons were interspersed with erratic attendance at a private school run by John T. Derry, a Confederate veteran, who called his institution a "selected classical institution." However, young Wilson would often accompany his father on walks through the city and visits to cotton mills and machine shops. Sunday afternoons were devoted to discussions of science and ideas, and often Joseph Wilson would have his son describe his observations in writing. For the rest of his life he remembered his father's insistence that "You do not know a subject until you can put it into the fewest and most expressive words." His grades at Derry's school were below average in Latin, history, bookkeeping, and writing, but at the same time his father insisted that he learn to think on his feet, as an orator must. On occasion father and son played chess or billiards, but cards were forbidden in that Presbyterian household.

These were the years during which the foundations of Woodrow Wilson's strong Presbyterian faith were laid, although his public profession of faith was delayed until his formal application for membership in the church after his father had moved on to Columbia, South Carolina, to teach at the theological seminary. The move was made in 1870, and in the once-lovely city still half-destroyed and now half jerry-rebuilt after Sherman's passage, Woodrow Wilson expressed the depths of his faith, found a personal hero, and began to develop ambitions.

His attendance at Mr. Barnwell's school in Columbia was of little more significance than that in Augusta, but his father and his uncle James Woodrow, who was also at the seminary, and his grandfather Woodrow, also living in Columbia, tutored him; at the same time, they felt strongly that his poor showing in school was somewhat disgraceful, and pondered his future. Young Wilson, Tommy to his family, had begun meanwhile to lead an active life of the imagination, perhaps as compensation for his few friends and comparatively inactive and lonely days.

Fed by the sea stories of Captain Frederick Marryat and James Fenimore Cooper, in his imagination he styled himself "Admiral Wilson," the commander of a fleet sent to destroy a gang of pirates. The series of reports which he wrote, ostensibly to the Navy Department, vividly described chases, battles, escapes, and problems that tested the admiral's seamanship. However, his interest in the sea waned as he began to develop his passion for the three interests that were to dominate his life: politics, religion, and education.

His interest in politics began when he discovered William Gladstone, the British Prime Minister, who became his hero and ultimately the inspiration for the political philosophy that dominated his first book, *Congressional Government*. His passion for Gladstone was largely the result of two growing interests, in public speaking and in a future political career. He was convinced that politics was the career in which he might best find personal fulfillment; at the same time he saw politics as the field in which he could best employ his speaking skill.

After reading about Gladstone's role in English parliamentary government in his father's copies of the *Edinburgh Review* and *The Nation*, Wilson became convinced that the parliamentary system was particularly suited to his interests in parliamentary procedure, debate, and persuasion. He found especially appealing Gladstone's *laissez-faire* political philosophy, particularly as it applied to economic policy and personal ability and ambition. Although both beliefs were later to change, his faith in the power of persuasion remained with him to the end, perhaps largely contributing to his later two major political failures in the presidency of Princeton and in the Presidency of the United States.

III *Religion*

During this period Wilson's lifelong Presbyterian faith began its long tenure as a major motivating force in his life and careers. Although he had long been considered normally religious within the family and indeed had participated in daily prayer and scripture reading, it appears that at sixteen, in Columbia, he experienced a genuine religious conversion, largely as the result of his closeness to Francis J. Brooke, a young seminarian who held frequent prayer meetings, at first in his room and later in the seminary chapel.

Although the specific details of that religious experience have never been recorded, years later, when Wilson as President of the United States visited the chapel, he said, "I feel as though I ought to take off my shoes. This is holy ground" (Baker, 1, 67). The records of the First Presbyterian Church state that "Thomas W. Wilson applied for Church membership" on July 5, 1873. The records state also that "three young men out of the Sunday school and well known to all of us," among whom was Wilson, applied for membership on that date and "after a free confession during which they severally exhibited evidences of a work of grace begun in their hearts, [they] were unanimously admitted to the membership of this church" (Baker, 1, 67). With this membership Wilson declared a faith that never wavered.

The substance of this faith was that of conservative Presbyterianism of the nineteenth century, the gospel according to John Calvin virtually unchanged since its implantation in Scottish character more than three hundred years before. At its center was a profound faith in a God who was both righteous and just, whose relationship with His faithful was both personal and direct. This relationship between man and God was based upon acceptance of the responsibility placed upon the individual by God and a determination to carry out that responsibility through faithfulness to conscience and to God's will.

Important, too, in this faith was the enhanced importance of those in whom God placed his trust, a belief firmly rooted in Calvin's concept of the Elect. To Wilson, faith, responsibility, and conscience were all signs of God's plan for him, and the result was a conviction of purpose that often bordered on the stubborn or the self-righteous. So convinced was he of his purpose that years later, when warned of the dangers of assassination, President Wilson declared, "Don't you know I am immortal 'till my work is done?"[3] Ultimately, too, he knew that he would be judged by God on the basis of the faithfulness with which that work was done. In later years he declared that only his belief in God enabled him to go on and to maintain his sanity.

This faith was tempered, nevertheless, by a strong, often sentimental romantic individualism philosophically related to Ralph Waldo Emerson's Transcendentalism. Self-reliance was for Wilson the foundation of all his opinions, actions, and principles, but they were not narrowly personal; they were extensions of God's will and wisdom and American destiny. Consequently, not only were retreat and surrender impossible for Wilson, but compromise inevitably meant not realistic acceptance of political practicality but weak rejection of moral absolutes. In the intensity of this faith the character of a great war President was forged; at the same time the seeds of personal tragedy were sown.

IV   Colleges

With his personal hero, personal faith, and personal ambitions clearly defined, Thomas Woodrow Wilson became, together with his friend Francis Brooke, a student at Davidson College in the fall of 1873. This small school at Piedmont, North Carolina, was founded to prepare boys of good but relatively poor families for the Presbyterian ministry, and apparently Wilson's family assumed that he was destined for that career. Although there is no record of his own attitude toward that family assumption, he began his education with interest and enthusiasm.

The lofty purpose of the college was reflected in its Spartan regimen. Wilson ate the sparse diet, pumped and hauled the communal water supply, and served on the stove committee. At the same time he played center field on the baseball team, perhaps because it was expected of him, and he belonged to the Emerson Literary Society, one of the school's two debating societies. His grades for the two terms of his attendance were close to average; he did consistently well in logic and rhetoric composition, and English, and less well in mathematics. His deportment was perfect.

The first year at Davidson was not an inauspicious beginning for a prospective Presbyterian minister, but it marked the end of his preministerial career. Apparently he spent much time worrying about his behavior prior to his conversion—years spent "in the service of the Devil"—and in the spring his health began to suffer. He

left the campus before the end of the term, suffering from an ailment
diagnosed as "nervous indigestion." This ailment would recur at
crucial times in his life until his White House physician, Navy
Lieutenant (later Admiral) Cary Grayson prescribed an antidote or
preventative essentially natural and psychological.

After leaving Davidson College, Wilson spent the following fifteen
months at Columbia, South Carolina, and later at Wilmington, North
Carolina, where his family moved in the fall of 1874. His purpose was
to prepare himself to enter Princeton College in New Jersey, then the
College of New Jersey, a school at which the sons of Presbyterian
ministers were welcome without the payment of tuition. At the same
time it was a Northern college considered suitable for young Southern gentlemen. Although Wilson's professional goals were not
clearly defined, his determination to do well at Princeton, his
increasing participation in debating groups, and his contributions to
the undergraduate magazine—articles on Otto von Bismarck and
William Pitt the Elder—suggest his continued and perhaps intensified interest in politics.

His grades improved so that his final four-year average was higher
than ninety percent. He followed British parliamentary debate in the
Gentlemen's Magazine, and he became speaker of the Whig Club,
managing editor of the *Princetonian,* and president of the baseball
association. As secretary of the Liberal Debating Club, he wrote the
organization's constitution, emphasizing a parliamentary structure,
whereby issues or bills were introduced, debated by the membership, and then voted upon by the membership.

V   *First Publication*

Wilson was not selected as one of the twenty-one "Honour Men" of
his class at the end of his freshman year, but by the end of his senior
year he was clearly one of the most widely known and respected
members of that class, largely as the result of his continued interest in
oratory and politics and the fact that his interests resulted in an essay,
"Cabinet Government in the United States," published in the
prestigious *International Review* in the issue of August 1879. The
junior editor who accepted it was Henry Cabot Lodge.

The argument advanced by Wilson in "Cabinet Government in the
United States" was the product of his interest in debate and in the
British parliamentary system, and it was to provide the foundation for

his book *Congressional Government*, which was to appear in 1885. It was also largely responsible for his personal leadership of academic causes as president of Princeton, his break with tradition in delivering personally messages to Congress as President of the United States, his personal role in peace negotiations, and his determination to win his version of the League of Nations over the reservations of Lodge and others. "Open covenants openly arrived at," his ultimate foundation of peace, was the logical extension of the open debate he saw as necessary in a society determined to be free. To Wilson, even as an undergraduate, the difference between open debate and secret agreement was obvious; decisions made in secret by politicians largely for their own benefit and without ultimate accountability militated against both the freedom and the prosperity of the nation; a cabinet modeled after the British system, growing out of a parliamentary political structure, would provide both the public accountability and the responsibility that the American system of congressional committees ignored.

Not only was the idea forcefully argued by the young writer, but it was well presented. Using carefully organized and effective rhetorical devices, Wilson first set up the immediacy with which the current situation demanded change by pointing out fears and dangers that are clear, present, and demanding:

> Our patriotism seems of late to have been exchanging its wonted tone of confident hope for one of desponding solicitude. Anxiety about the future of our institutions seems to be daily becoming stronger in the minds of thoughtful Americans. A feeling of uneasiness is undoubtedly prevalent, sometimes taking the shape of a fear that grave, perhaps radical, defects in our mode of government are militating against our liberty and prosperity. A marked and alarming decline in statesmanship, a rule of levity and folly instead of wisdom and sober forethought in legislation, threaten to shake our trust not only in the men by whom our national policy is controlled, but also in the very principles upon which our government rests. Both State and National legislatures are looked upon with nervous suspicion, and we hail an adjournment of Congress as a temporary immunity from danger. . . .[4]

Writing in the aftermath of Andrew Johnson's impeachment, of the Grant administration, of Credit Mobilier and panic, of the partisan and extralegal resolution of the disputed election of 1876, and of a Reconstruction and occupation prolonged for more than a decade— and also under the influence of his British legislative ideal—Wilson identified the source of fear and uncertainty in precise terms:

What is the real cause of this solicitude and doubt? It is, in our opinion, to be found in the absorption of all power by a legislature which is practically irresponsible for its acts. . . . Nothing can be more obvious than the fact that the very life of free, popular institutions is dependent upon their breathing the bracing air of thorough, exhaustive, and open discussions, or that select Congressional committees, whose proceedings must from their very nature be secret, are, as means of legislation, dangerous and unwholesome. (Baker-Dodd I, I, 20–21)

The solution to this denial of a free and open exchange of ideas was obvious to Wilson; the Founding Fathers had not only separated powers of government, but had isolated them into mutually suspicious entities. Hostilities might be removed, gaps bridged and openness achieved by his plan: "Simply to give the heads of the Executive departments—the members of the Cabinet—seats in Congress, with the privilege of the initiative in legislation and some part of the unbounded privileges now commanded by the Standing Committees . . ." (Baker-Dodd I, I, 25). With branches linked and power and responsibility mutually shared, openness would be inevitable and freedom would be preserved.

Particularly evident in Wilson's article are the immediacy of the danger and the logic of the solution, a solution whose time, he was convinced, had come and whose delay might be fatal. Evident too is the maturity of a prose style that Wilson had done much to perfect in the course of his education by his father at home and to a great extent by himself and his peers at Princeton. In spite of the exaggerated dangers inherent in the existing system as well as in delayed change—exaggerations born perhaps of ideological zeal and impatient youth—evidence is clear that Wilson possessed a clear mind, a devotion to openness, and a passion for reform.

Equally evident in other writings of Wilson's undergraduate years is his growing interest in practical politics and in the desirable characteristics of both politics and politicians, all of which was dominated by a faith in openness, honesty, and the wisdom inherent in a society made up of an informed electorate and virtuous leaders. Thus, as a sophomore, writing in "Prince Bismarck" in the *Princetonian,* he defined ideal statesmen as "men of independent conviction, full of self-trust, and themselves the spirit of their country's institutions" (Baker-Dodd I, I, 6). Statesmanship he defined "as being that resolute and vigorous advance towards the realization of high, definite, and consistent aims which issues from the unreserved devotion of a strong intellect to the service of the state

and to the solution of all the multiform problems of public policy . . ." (Baker-Dodd I, I, 68–69). The eloquence of this conviction
in his Nassau prize essay, "William, Earl of Chatham," might well be
prefatory to his war message to Congress on April 2, 1917.

Other essays in the *Princetonian* reflect the foundations of ideas,
policies, and convictions of the future. In writing of Gladstone he
defined the political mind succinctly:

> Great statesmen seem to direct and rule by a sort of power to put
> themselves in the place of the nation over whom they are set, and may thus be
> said to possess the souls of poets at the same time that they display the coarser
> sense and the more vulgar society of men of business. (Baker-Dodd I, I,
> 68–69)

Further indication of the course of future events and policies
appears in his appreciation of John Richard Green's *Short History of
the English People,* the result of a profound impact; the book
obviously influenced his attitude toward the American people, its
origins and its institutions, as he was to reveal it in his own
multivolume history a quarter-century later. The undergraduate of
1872 foreshadowed the philosophy of history of the university
professor of 1902 as he wrote: "It is a grateful thought that this *History
of the English People* is a history of the American people as well, it is a
high and solemn thought that we, as a lusty branch of a noble race, are
by our national history adding lustre or stain to so bright an
escutcheon" (Baker I, 96).

During these undergraduate years the foundations of Wilson's
forceful prose and his political philosophy were laid, and, superim-
posed on his profound religious faith, those characteristics were to
point the way toward a future dominated by idealism, determination,
and self-confidence. Thus, when he left Princeton in 1879 he was
confident of a political career on the highest levels, and he determined to study law as a means to that end.

CHAPTER 2

The Search for a Profession

I   The Law

ALTHOUGH his family still saw him as a future Presbyterian minster, Wilson convinced them that he should study law. A practical balance to his already substantial grasp of political theory, the study of law would also provide a basis for the political leadership to which he aspired. With cool clarity, four years later he described his plan at the time to his fiancée, Ellen Axson: "The profession I chose was politics; the profession I entered was the law. I entered the one because I thought it would lead to the other. It was once the sure road; and Congress is still full of lawyers" (Baker I, 109).

With this plan firmly in mind "Thomas W. Wilson" entered the University of Virginia at Charlottesville on October 2, 1879, and he entered that signature in the Bursar's Record. A year later he signed the record "T. Woodrow Wilson," and shortly thereafter the initial disappeared forever. Although Freud and Bullitt make much of the psychological implications of this shift—alleging an unsuccessful love affair, rejection, dropping the name of the love object's father (his first name, Thomas, but not Woodrow, his last)—the evidence suggests that for one who had signed his name countless times in dozens of imagined political roles, and particularly for one who was fascinated by the rhythms of language and literary style, it was without question a natural, uncomplicated step. Furthermore, Freud and Bullitt do not have the facts quite straight. He wrote T. Woodrow Wilson in the register in the fall of 1880, but Harriet Woodrow did not refuse his proposal until summer 1881.

Wilson brought with him to Virginia the reputation as a productive, promising student that he had acquired as a Princeton undergraduate, and in his little more than a year at the university he added to that reputation. Although not an athlete, he umpired games and supported the teams; he joined Phi Kappa Psi and the Jefferson

Society, of which he became president; he became a champion orator and debater, and, as he had been so often before, a supporter and the chief framer of a new constitution for the Society. A frequent contributor to the *University of Virginia Magazine,* he continued his conscious pursuit of a unique, forceful, and persuasive literary style. He did well in his courses.

Two of his activities give much insight into the course of Wilson's life and thought during his brief preparation for the law: his key speech on the negative side of the Jefferson Society debate on the question "Is the Roman Catholic Element in the United States a Menace to American Institutions?" and his contribution of "Mr. Gladstone—A Character Sketch" to the *University of Virginia Magazine.* The debate was not only the performance for which he was named the Society's outstanding orator, although he lost the debate, but its substance indicated a definite broadening of the outlook and increase in the tolerance of the small-town Presbyterian minister's son from the South, thus, perhaps, laying the foundation for his later close relationship with his secretary and biographer, Joseph P. Tumulty. The sketch on Gladstone not only extended his regard for the statesman but also made clear the ultimate source of his admiration: the rigid moral sense of a Christian statesman.

When Wilson spoke on John Bright, the British statesman who had opposed British recognition of the Confederacy—still a touchy subject in Virginia in 1880—the hall was crowded, and Wilson carried the audience with him as he declaimed: "I yield to no one precedence in love for the South. . . . But because I love the South, I rejoice in the failure of the Confederacy. Suppose that secession had been accomplished? . . . Even the damnable cruelty and folly of recon-struction were to be preferred to helpless independence."[1]

Although Wilson confessed that the law bored him, his activities were considered brilliant, and the university library records show that his reading interests were largely in history, oratory, political biography, and poetry (he kept Shelley's *Poems* so long overdue that he was fined fifty cents). At the end of his first year he planned to continue his law studies, but two factors combined to alter his plans: the unfortunate love affair with his cousin Harriet Woodrow, daugh-ter of his uncle Thomas, and another siege of the ill health that had forced him to leave Davidson. The former was even to lead him in the summer of 1881 to plan to establish himself in Chillicothe, Ohio, Harriet's home town, there to read and practice law, but her refusal of his proposal of marriage turned his attention farther South. The illness—digestive and nervous problems—forced Wilson, in December 1880, to leave the University of Virginia. With the exception of his summer 1881 visit to Chillicothe, he spent the next twenty months at home in Wilmington, where he finished his studies and received his degree *in absentia*. He also spent a great deal of time tutoring his younger brother and reading for pleasure. He then began to think of the practice of law.

Atlanta, Georgia, in 1882 saw itself in the image drawn for it by Henry W. Grady, and it was in this self-styled capital of the New South that Wilson determined to establish his law practice. Admitted to the Georgia Bar in October 1882, he set up an office with Edward I. Renick, a University of Virginia friend. But Atlanta had attracted one lawyer for every 270 people, and the firm of Renick and Wilson did not prosper. His first two clients were a court-assigned client and his mother.

As at Princeton and Charlottesville, his successes were largely extracurricular: although he wrote that "hereabout, culture is very little esteemed," he tried to start a debating club which he meant to call the "Georgia House of Commons," for which he began to write a constitution; he testified before the United States Tariff Commission, Atlanta session, in favor of free trade; and he then started an Atlanta branch of the Free Trade Club. He read Walter Bagehot's *The English Constitution;* in the editor of the *Economist* he had a new hero, and he planned a similar American study.

Improved in health, Wilson grew new side whiskers, and in April 1883, in Rome, Georgia, he met Ellen Axson, daughter of the Reverend Edward Axson, pastor of Rome's First Presbyterian Church. He fell promptly in love, but, having been refused once and perhaps twice, troubled in beginning a career and beginning to think of a change, he was reluctant to pursue her. Impatiently returning to his slow-starting career, he wrote what was to become the first chapter of *Congressional Government.* As an article it was rejected by *The Nation.* An article on Georgia's convict lease system was rejected by the *New York Evening Post*, and in the fall of 1883 he abandoned the law.

II *Academia*

Determined to become a professor—the law practice had taught him that he was too impatient of legal tedium to be successful in practice and that his interests were largely in theory and in persuasion—he applied unsuccessfully to Johns Hopkins University for a fellowship. Then, with his father's financial support, he entered Johns Hopkins in the fall of 1883. A year later he became a "Historical Fellow." He studied in Professor Herbert Baxter Adams's history seminar, and he continued interest in extracurricular affairs, joining the glee club and the Hopkins Literary Society, which he transformed into the Hopkins House of Commons, a forum for debate. In January 1884 his article "Committee or Cabinet Government," written in Atlanta, was published in the *Overland Monthly,* and he wrote "An Old Master," a study of Adam Smith, later published in his first collection of essays. In both articles he indicated that his early political faith in the efficiency and effectiveness of cabinet government and in the moral rightness of free trade and free enterprise were undiminished, and he began to write his best-known, widely read, and controversial study, *Congressional Government.*

At the same time Wilson was moving closer to marriage with Ellen Axson. He had visited her in Rome in the summer of 1883 and later that summer, on his way to Baltimore, he stopped in Asheville, North Carolina, where she was visiting. There he proposed to her and was accepted. Although their visits were brief during the two years of Wilson's stay at Johns Hopkins, their betrothal was marked by the exchange of long, romantic, often wistful letters. They planned to marry when Wilson's studies were completed and he had found a teaching job.

Although Wilson had changed the means by which he was to earn his living and find his entry into a political career, it is evident that he had not abandoned his ultimate goal. Rather, as he wrote in October 1883:

Whoever thinks, as I thought, that he can practice law successfully and study history and politics at the same time is woefully mistaken. If he is to make a living at the bar he must be a lawyer *and nothing else.* Of course he can compass a certain sort of double-calling success by dint of dishonesty. He can obtain, and betray, clients by pretending a knowledge of the law which he does not possess; and he can often gain political office by the arts of the demagogue. But he cannot be both a learned lawyer and a profound and public-spirited statesman, if he must plunge into practice and make the law a means of support. (Baker I, 158)

Still determined to dedicate himself to a life of "profound and public-spirited statesmanship" but to change the direction by which to approach that career, nevertheless he scaled down his ambitions from practical political leader to political philosopher and litterateur:

What I have wished to emphasize is the *object* for which I came to the University: to get a special training in historical research and an insight into the most modern literary and political thoughts and methods, in order that my ambition to become an invigorating and enlightening power in the world of political thought and a master in some of the less serious branches of literary art may be the more easy of accomplishment. (Baker I, 168)

Wilson chose Johns Hopkins because it was an intellectually exciting institution, "the best place in America to study" (Baker I, 173), but at the same time he determined to maintain his own intellectual independence, and in the informality of the Adams Historical Seminar of which he became "scribe," he found the stimulation to develop his own work. After Adams's death in 1902 he wrote that "his head was a veritable clearing house of ideas in the field of historical study. . . . The thesis work done under him may fairly be said to have set the pace for university work in history throughout the United States" (Baker I, 179).

Of most importance to Wilson was the freedom given him by Adams to carry on his own research and writing. "He received my confidences with sympathy, readily freed me from his 'institutional' work, and bade me go on with my 'constitutional' studies, promising me all the aid and encouragement he could give me, and saying that the work I proposed was just such as he wanted to see done" (Baker I, 180). The result was that Wilson was delighted to read portions of *Congressional Government* aloud to the seminar, thus gaining perspective from the discussion of his work by Adams and a group that included Richard T. Ely, J. Franklin Jameson, Albert Shaw, and a number of other bright young men who were destined for distinction.

Wilson's letters to his fiancée during this exciting, stimulating, and productive year are not only romantic but intensely revealing, especially of his search for the disciplinary basis of sustained work, a problem that had never before confronted or interested him. Thus, although in November 1883 he wrote Ellen that "my chief ground of indictment against my professors here is that they give a man infinitely more than he can digest. If I were not discreet enough to refuse many of the things set before me, my mental digestion would soon be utterly ruined" (Baker I, 182), nevertheless, a year later he wrote that "there is a sort of grim satisfaction, in tiring one's mind out, if it be only to prove one's mastery over natural disinclinations" (Baker I, 183). Nevertheless, he concluded that "if a man does not find duty agreeable, he does not deserve gratification" (Baker I, 183).

Also evident in this series of letters is the continuation of Wilson's concern with the development of his literary style. Shortly after his arrival at Johns Hopkins he wrote Ellen:

> Style is not much studied here; *ideas* are supposed to be everything—their vehicle comparatively nothing. But you and I know that there can be no greater mistake; that both in its amount and in its length of life an author's influence depends upon the power and the beauty of his style; upon the flawless perfection of the mirror he holds up to nature; upon his facility in catching and holding because he pleases, the attention: and style shall be, as under my father's guidance, one of my chief studies. A writer must be artful as well as strong. (Baker I, 184)

His concern with his stylistic development continued, as he wrote later that "I know that my careful compositions of today are vastly better than I could have written five, or even three years ago . . . but what is my style to what it should be!" (Baker I, 184), and later, after listening to a lecture by Edmund Gosse, "the worst of listening to a style like Gosse's is that it makes one so desperately dissatisfied with one's own" (Baker I, 184). Pleased by favorable comments on the style of "Cabinet or Committee Government" when it appeared in the *Overland Monthly,* nevertheless he commented that "I'm sure I can write much better prose than that . . ." (Baker I, 186).

Although bothered by recurring attacks of illness, at least once returning to Wilmington to recuperate, Wilson was determined that he should complete his studies as quickly as possible so that he and his fiancée might marry when he found a suitable job. Nevertheless his preoccupation with his extracurricular activities—the glee club, the debating society, which he reorganized and for which he provided a constitution, and close attention to visiting lecturers ranging from Gosse to Henry Ward Beecher—continued; he drew up a list of aids to pronunciation of English largely from usage for Miss Axson; and he began to develop an interest in art, paralleling that interest of Ellen's. He attended the theater on occasion, particularly enjoying the Ellen Terry-Henry Irving production of *Hamlet,* and yet continued his intensely personal relationship with the Presbyterian Chruch and with his God.

While Wilson was at Johns Hopkins the growing theological battle between fundamentalism and modernism became personal for him with the charges of heresy brought against his uncle, James Woodrow. "God's word and His works cannot be antagonistic" (Baker 1, 210), he wrote in his uncle's defense, and upon his uncle's suspension from his duties in the Chair of Science and Religion, Wilson wrote, "What *is* to become of our dear church! She has indeed fallen upon evil times of ignorance and folly!" (Baker 1, 210).

At the same time, during this period of intense activity in many areas, Wilson continued writing *Congressional Government*, and he began his collaboration with Richard T. Ely in writing *The History of American Economic Thought*. Nevertheless, Wilson's critics insist that he learned very little at Johns Hopkins, pointing particularly to his criticism of the school and its professors and to the continuity of thought between "Cabinet Government in the United States," written in his senior year at Princeton, and *Congressional Government*, written largely at Hopkins, for their evidence.[2] At the same time, supporters, most notably Ray Stannard Baker, insist that it was one of his most influential as well as productive periods, making a record of "extraordinary brilliance" (Baker 1, 234). The truth lies somewhere in between. Wilson's motivation in attending Hopkins was less than that of the student eagerly drinking at the fountain of knowledge and more the young man preparing for a coolly chosen career. Nevertheless, it was a successful two years from both points of view, and, although he decided to forego finishing the work for his Ph.D., choosing to leave at the end of two years, he was offered another fellowship for the following year; he had been asked by G. Stanley Hall to assist him in logic and philosophy; and possible job opportunities began to appear, most of them the result of his professors' recommendations. Although Ellen urged him to finish work on his degree, his father's advice reinforced his own inclination to choose his own reading and studies, thus foregoing the requirements. The author of a successful book, the ardent suitor, and the young man belatedly finding his profession, Wilson was eager to be at work and to be married. Although the following year he submitted *Congressional Government* as his thesis and took the examinations at the urging of Ellen and his new employer, he manifested little interest in the degree either personally or intellectually.

When he was awarded the degree in 1886, the result of circumstances not unlike his self-study for his law degree at Virginia, he was possessed of a growing reputation as a political scientist, and he was associate professor of history at the newly established Bryn Mawr

College. Perhaps more importantly he and Ellen Axson had been
married in the Manse of the Independent Presbyterian Church in
Savannah, Georgia, the home of her grandfather. Significantly,
although Wilson considered his studies at Johns Hopkins complete,
his fiancée gave up her art studies uncompleted. From the time of
their marriage until her death in the White House on August 6, 1914,
her role throughout the course of their marriage was to provide him
with a stability and direction that he had not known before; his
recurring illness and occasional despondence, particularly in tests of
leadership and conviction in later years at Princeton and in Trenton,
were largely relieved by her presence and stability, and even as she
became progressively weaker in her last years, at the same time she
did much to dissipate his gloom, which came more and more
frequently. More than anything else, she gave his life focus and
direction.

CHAPTER 3

The Young Professor

I Congressional Government

THE first major result of Wilson's career as a scholar-educator, *Congressional Government* remains the most durable and the best known. The product of his distaste for the American system of separate legislative and executive powers, it reflects most clearly his admiration for Walter Bagehot and his *English Constitution* (for a time he covered Gladstone's picture in his room with that of Bagehot), for his concern with clear governmental lines of leadership, authority, and control, and for the role of open discussion in arriving at political decisions made in full view of the public.

At the same time *Congressional Government* clearly reflects its origin in the times out of which it came. In the previous twenty years the American constitutional union had been shaken by antislavery controversy, Civil War, and Reconstruction, largely the result of constitutional ambiguity and leadership uncertainties. The institution of the Presidency had become strengthened to meet crisis, largely through power assumed by a strong President, only to be weakened by assassination and impeachment. With Lincoln dead and Johnson discredited, the Presidency had not only been weakened by a series of reluctant or inept Presidents, but also by the scandals that reached into the White House under Ulysses S. Grant and the shadow under which Rutherford B. Hayes took office. Most immediately, Hayes had been succeeded by James A. Garfield, whose reputation had been clouded and whose tenure was abruptly ended by Charles Guiteau's bullet and a lingering and fatal illness. His successor, Chester A. Arthur, the occupant of the While House and the Presidency during which Wilson wrote *Congressional Government*, was a man of little influence or power and of flawed reputation. During these years, Wilson's formative years as a young Southerner, a student, and an emerging scholar and political philosopher, the central power in American government rested not in the White House but at the opposite end of Pennsylvania Avenue. During many of these years, protective tariffs, disputed electoral results, and railroad and Wall Street–related scandals suggested that the congressional oligarchy had become not only the dominant force in American political life but the ultimate corrupter of the democratic ideal.

Given this set of circumstances it was perhaps inevitable that Wilson should begin with the assumption that the weak Presidency and strong Congress was a permanent condition, an assumption that he was to refute in the preface to the fifteenth edition, written and published in 1900. As he points out in that preface, *Congressional Government* described the American political reality at the time it was written; it did not attempt to be prophetic.

With the evidence of the times clearly in mind, Wilson made his intention clear to Ellen Axson. On January 1, 1884, he wrote:

I've opened the new year by a day of diligent work on my favorite constitutional studies. I've planned a set of four or five essays on "The Government of the Union," in which my purpose is to show, as well as I can, our constitutional system as it looks in operation. My desire and ambition are to treat the American constitution as Mr. Bagehot (do you remember Mr. Bagehot, about whom I talked to you one night on the veranda at Asheville?) has treated the English Constitution. His book has inspired my whole study of our government. He brings to the work a fresh and original method, which has made the British system much more intelligible to ordinary men than it ever was before, and which, if it could be successfully applied to the exposition of our Federal constitution, would result in something like a revelation to those who are still reading the *Federalist* as an authoritative constitutional manual. . . . (Baker 1, 213–14)

With mock modesty Wilson suggested that his goal was perhaps beyond his capabilities; nevertheless, his plan was to define the reality as well as how it had come about:

. . . I've been writing . . . an historical sketch of the modifications which have been wrought in the federal system and which have resulted in making Congress the omnipotent power in the government, to the overthrow of the checks and balances to be found in the "literary theory." This is to serve as an introduction to essays upon Congress itself, in which I wish to examine at length the relations of Congress to the Executive and that legislative machinery which contains all the springs of federal action. (Baker 1, 214–15)

Congressional Government follows the plan that Wilson so clearly outlined to Miss Axson. The "Introductory" portion defines, first of all, the constitutional ideal and reality as Wilson saw it; the Consitution, he says, is *"our form of government* rather in name than in reality, the form of the Constitution being one of nicely adjusted, ideal balances, whilst the actual form of our present government is simply a scheme of congressional supremacy . . .";[1] the result of machination, evolution, and manipulation, as the powers have sought supremacy that defies balance, is, in practice "a government by the Standing Committee of Congress."[2] The reason, then, for his study, is made clear:

. . . As the House of Commons is the central object of examination in every study of the English Constitution, so should Congress be in every study of our own. Anyone who is unfamiliar with what Congress actually does and how it does it, with all its duties and all its occupations, with all its devices of management and resources of power, is very far from a knowledge of the constitutional system under which we live; and to every one who knows these things that knowledge is very near.[3]

The work proper is divided into four discussion essays and a conclusion. The first two essays focus upon the House of Representatives, whereas, significantly, the Senate and the Executive branch are each discussed in one essay. This division makes clear Wilson's view of the nature and structure of the American government as he saw it. The House, or more properly, the Standing Committees of the House, are the centers of power in his view of the federal system, and the Senate functions as an American House of Lords, a body that checks the democratic enthusiasms of the House. The Executive branch, on the other hand, is responsible for carrying out the will of Congress. In the House, it was evident to Wilson that

the leaders of the House are the chairmen of the principal Standing Committees. Indeed, to be exactly accurate, the House has as many leaders as there are subjects of legislation. . . . It is this multiplicity of leaders, this many-headed leadership, which makes the organization of the House too complex to afford uninformed people and unskilled observers any easy clue to its methods of rule. . . . It is impossible to discover any unity or method in the disconnected and therefore unsystematic, confused, and desultory action of the House, or any common purpose in the measures which its committees from time to time recommend.[4]

As confused and confusing as this system appears to be to the outsider, Wilson insists that it is equally confusing to the newly elected Congressman, who easily becomes disgusted, dispirited, and, if he remains, eventually a helpless cog in the mechanism, his voice unheard and his programs lost in the morass of committee government. In England and France, Wilson insists, parties speak with a single voice; here party principles are often sacrificed to the expediencies made mandatory by the composition of committees.

Particularly complex and confusing as well as often counterproductive is, in Wilson's view, the committee structure of Congress as it applies to the power of taxation and expenditure, the subject of his second essay. Especially appalling to Wilson is the fact that

the national income is controlled by one Committee of the House and one of the Senate; the expenditures of the government are regulated by fifteen Committees of the House and five of the Senate; and the currency is cared for by two Committees of the House and one of the Senate; by all of which it appears that the financial administration of the country is in the hands of twenty-four Committees of Congress. . . .[5]

The Congress, as it appears to Wilson, is a body constantly at odds with itself, structured in a way most conducive to self-serving, to corruption, and to perpetuating itself in office and in power at the expense of honesty, responsibility, and efficiency in government. Again, for Wilson, the British governmental structure, marked by the openness of Parliamentary debate, the consistency of party positions, and the central role of responsibility and accountability provide a system at once efficient and honest.

In moving on to the examination of the Senate, Wilson draws a further parallel between the two systems: although both have similar functions—as exalted bodies functioning as preservers of tradition— the American Senate has the hitherto unrealized potential of providing the leadership Congress has lacked except in such crises of the past as marked the emergence of Daniel Webster and a handful of others. Nevertheless, Wilson asserts, our very political structure makes it difficult for such men to appear:

It is . . . very unfortunate that only feeling or enthusiasm can create recognized leadership in our politics. There is no office set apart for the great party leader in our government. The powers of the Speakership of the House of Representatives are too limited in scope; the presidency is too silent and inactive, too little like a premiership and too much like a superintendency. If there be any one man to whom a whole party or a great national majority looks for guiding counsel, he must lead without office, as Daniel Webster did, or in spite of his office, as Jefferson and Jackson did.[6]

These men, and others like them, led because, as Wilson had long believed, "It is natural that orators should be the leaders of a self-governing people."[7] And, as the Senate is organized to function much as does the House, the role for such a leader is limited. Although some senators become prominent, each remains, Wilson insists, merely a Senator, never *the* Senator, the spokesman for his party or the voice of his government.

The executive function of government is, to Wilson, just that, and the role of the President is that of the executor of congressional legislation rather than that of a party or national leader in his own right. The talent required for the Presidency is that of the administrator, and consequently, "For the sort of President needed under the present arrangement of our federal government, it is best to choose amongst the ablest and most experienced state governors";[8] he then chooses, with senatorial advice and consent, a cabinet whose members are largely responsible for the operation of the executive branch, and he himself is "no greater than his prerogative of veto makes him. . . ."[9] Wilson concludes that "every government is largely what the men are who constitute it";[10] thus far men have made it the awkward, imbalanced, unresponsive mechanism that we know.

In his summation Wilson concludes that evidence suggests the courage necessary to continue the study of government will also prove to be the courage necessary to bring about necessary change:

> The Constitution is not honored by blind worship. The more open-eyed we become, as a nation, to its defects, and the prompter we grow in applying with the unhesitating courage of conviction all thoroughly-tested or well-considered expedients necessary to make self-government among us a straightforward thing of simple method, single, unstinted power, and clear responsibility, the nearer will we approach to the sound sense and practical genius of the great and honorable statesmen of 1787.[11]

Again, as Wilson's critics are eager to point out, the implications are clear: study will lead to constitutional change, and such change will inevitably lead us closer to the British Parliamentary ideal as Wilson perceived it in his study of Gladstone and Bagehot:

> When we shall have examined all its parts without sentiment, and gauged

all its functions by the standards of practical common sense, we shall have established anew our right to the claim of political sagacity; and it will remain only to act intelligently upon what our opened eyes have seen in order to prove again the justice of our claim to political genius.[12]

Wilson's conclusions about the nature of American constitutional government were not only the result of his interest in oratory and persuasion and his admiration for the British system of open debate and parliamentary responsibility, but they are also the product of the post–Civil War experience, particularly from the Southern point of view. The history of the Presidency, from the impeachment of President Johnson through the ineptitudes of the two Grant administrations, the scandals, and the corruption of what Mark Twain aptly styled the "Gilded Age," is essentially the history of the decline of the power and prestige of the Presidency. At the same time it is the history of the growth of the alliance between Northern Republicans and Southern Democratic members of Congress that not only brought an end to Reconstruction but also gave a free hand to the country's new economic barons as it awarded the Presidency to Rutherford B. Hayes, the second member of the parade of Civil War generals to the White House. As Wilson wrote, it appeared that the condition was permanent, that Congress would no longer permit the ascendancy of a Lincoln, a Jackson, or a Jefferson, and consequently, if the power of the people and their right to know what went on in Congress were to be protected, a reconstruction of the legislative branch, to make its members responsive and responsible, was necessary. The model of the British system was for Wilson perhaps more a convenience than an object of the mindless adulation that some critics insist that it was.

These same critics point out in support of their position that Wilson, writing in Baltimore, a short distance from Washington, nevertheless did not bother to go there to observe Congress in action, to support his conclusions with the firsthand evidence that he might have gathered. However, Wilson's concern was not with a day, a week, or even an entire session; he was concerned with generalities based upon two decades and five Presidencies, a period of time that could hardly be verified or refuted by a day's observations.

II   *The Beginning of Change*

However, even as Wilson was writing, the forces of change were beginning to make themselves felt. In November 1884, while Wilson was preparing the manuscript for the press, Grover Cleveland, the first Democratic President since James Buchanan, was elected, and he took office on March 5, while Wilson was looking for a job and preparing to marry Ellen Axson. Because Wilson does not insist in his conclusion upon the necessity of converting the American congressional system to something approximating the parliamentary system, contenting himself with the statement that he was "pointing out facts, diagnosing, not prescribing remedies,"[13] it is possible to conclude, as has Walter Lippmann,[14] that Wilson, who had supported Cleveland, anticipated the possibility that Cleveland might restore the dignity and perhaps some of the power of the Presidency. Such a conclusion is attractive, but not only is there no direct evidence to support it, as Lippmann admits, but the absence of evidence to support that conclusion is more suggestive of the opposite: that although Wilson, as a Southern Democrat, supported Cleveland as a matter of course, even perhaps out of a sense of political justice, he had no real hope or belief that Cleveland might wrestle power out of the hands of Congress and move the Presidency toward ascendancy. Rather, as Wilson saw it as he concluded *Congressional Government,* the path of American government and the centrality of American political power in the Congress seemed fixed.

Nevertheless *Congressional Government* is a major work that demonstrates most conclusively and forcefully the inevitable result of the American constitutional system in a period of congressional supremacy. Central to such a time is the diffusion of responsibility that Wilson describes when the Presidency refuses or is unable to lead. Not only is responsibility distorted, but the very processes of government become the province of a few powerful men functioning in political secrecy. As Lippmann comments, this was a good book to have read during the Harding administration, at the end of the Truman administration and the beginning of the Eisenhower administration, and during the McCarthy era.[15] It is also a good book to have read during the period that began with the assassination of John F. Kennedy, carried through the assault that drove Lyndon Johnson from the Presidency, and then confused the person of the President with the office of the Presidency during the administration of Richard Nixon. As a study of the nature of its subject, *Congressional Government* is a permanent plea for the nature of government as it was designed by those who, more than a hundred years before, had attempted to emulate the functioning of the universe as the Enlightenment saw it to be. Although Wilson's cure for imbalance was made obsolete by the passage of time and the accession to the Presidency of strong men, including Wilson himself, nevertheless, the observations are sound, with or without a tour of the halls and committee rooms of Congress.

For a first book, *Congressional Government* is both forceful and confident, each to an extent that offended some of his critics. The book was well received and it is still read, not only because of the practical object-lesson and record that it is, but because it is evidence that Wilson had learned well the lessons in persuasion that his father had begun. Wilson's prose is mannered and precise; it is smooth and clear. Occasional lapses into near-pedantry are few, and none is serious enough to mar it. In *The Nation* for February 12, 1885—less than a month before Grover Cleveland took office—Gamaliel Bradford described it in a eulogistic review as:

one of the most important books, dealing with political subjects, which have ever been issued from the American press. We have often been asked by students of politics and by foreign visitors for some book which would explain the real working of our Government, and have been obliged to confess that there was none in existence. Of those which explain the origin of the Constitution, the intentions of its framers, and the meaning of its provisions, the name is legion; but of what the Government established by it has actually become after a century of history, if there is any expositor, it has escaped our search. . . . This want Mr. Wilson has come forward to supply. . . . (Baker I, 223)

In this and other reviews there is no suggestion that Wilson was describing a governmental phenomenon already passing; it was seen as breaking new ground in critical political philosophy; widely translated, it was quoted as authoritative by James Bryce in his *American Commonwealth*; and in 1892 it won Johns Hopkins University's John Marshall Prize. *Congressional Government* made Wilson, at twenty-eight, an important figure in American political thought and in higher education. Without exaggeration, it can be asserted that his first book not only made possible Wilson's accession to the presidency of Princeton University but led him ultimately to the Presidency of the nation.

Nevertheless, fifteen years later, when Wilson as professor of Jurisprudence and Politics at Princeton University was asked to write a preface for the fifteenth printing of the book, he commented in detail on the changes that had taken place in the intricate interrelationships of American government: the numbers of Congressmen had increased, as had the numbers of the standing committees of both House and Senate. The Tenure of Office Act, which had led to Johnson's impeachment, first became inoperative and then was repealed. More economic power had passed to the Secretary of the Treasury; the office of the Speaker of the House of Representatives had evolved into a concentrated leadership. However, the war with Spain had contributed greatly to the increasing power of the Presidency, a power that Wilson saw as continuing to grow. These conclusions led him to write his later *Constitutional Government.*

Nevertheless, in 1885 *Congressional Government* was responsible for Wilson's new prominence, for his appointment as associate professor of History and Political Economy at Bryn Mawr College, the appointment that made his marriage possible, and it was responsible for a new closeness between Wilson and his father, to whom it had been dedicated, a new relationship of which Freud and Bullitt make a great deal. But its real importance rested in the validity of his observations and the clarity and confidence with which he reported them.

With his marriage and his first academic appointment, it appeared that the course of Wilson's life was set, not in terms of his early political ambitions, although he had never renounced them, but as that of an analyst and teacher, a theorist rather than a leader. Woodrow Wilson, at the age of twenty-eight, had become a schoolmaster.

CHAPTER 4

The Successful Scholar

WITH such an auspicious beginning of his academic career, Woodrow Wilson nevertheless accepted it as less than he had hoped for. Although he wrote Ellen Axson that "most men of my age and in the earliest, most critical stages of their careers would be willing to pay any price for such a notice from such a paper as the *Nation*, and would enjoy very keenly such congratulations as it has brought me" (Baker I, 227), and had resigned himself to making his political power felt through literary rather than partisan persuasion, he also wrote his fiancée that

there is, and has long been, in my mind a "lurking sense of disappointment and *loss*, as if I had missed from my life something upon which both my gifts and inclinations gave me a claim;" I do feel a very real regret, that I have been shut out from my heart's *first*—primary—ambition and purpose, which was, to take an active, if possible a leading, part in public life, and strike out for myself if I had the ability, a statesman's career. That is my heart's—or, rather, my *mind's*—deepest secret. . . . But don't mistake the feeling for more than it is. It is nothing *more* than a regret; and the more I study the conditions of public service in this country, the less *personal* does the regret become. My disappointment is in the fact that there is no room for such a career in this country for *anybody*, rather than in the fact that there is no chance for *me*. Had I had independent means of support, even of the most modest proportions, I should doubtless have sought an entrance into politics *anyhow*, and have tried to fight my way to predominant influence even amidst the hurly-burly and helter-skelter of Congress. I have a strong instinct of leadership, an unmistakable oratorical temperament, and the keenest possible delight in affairs; and it has required very constant and stringent schooling to content me with the sober methods of the scholar and the man of letters. I have no patience for the tedious toil of what is known as "research"; I have a passion for interpreting great thoughts to the world; I should be complete if I could inspire a great movement of opinion, if I could read the experiences of the past into the practical life of the men of to-day and so communicate the thought to the minds of the great mass of the people as to impel them to great political achievements. . . . (Baker I, 228–29)

48

To Wilson it was clear that he had bowed to the inevitable and accepted the lesser course, but there is no suggestion in his comments of the time that in beginning an academic career he was entering a field dominated by the very techniques and attitudes that he thought were forever behind him. On June 24, 1885, he married Ellen Axson at her grandfather's home in Savannah, and after a two-week honeymoon in North Carolina, they visited relatives until September, when they established themselves at Bryn Mawr, outside Philadelphia.

Wilson's years at Bryn Mawr were neither happy nor greatly productive. The college was beginning its first year when Wilson joined the faculty. The campus consisted of two buildings and the first class of forty-two young ladies; three frame houses, each with its cook-housekeeper, housed the faculty, and Wilson's traditional educational technique, based upon the formal lecture, clashed with the innovative discussion technique favored by Dean Martha Thomas. Furthermore he was basically unsympathetic to the kind of education for women to which Bryn Mawr was dedicated. He spent a good deal of time preparing his lectures; he completed his Ph.D. in 1886; and he took long walks in the hills.

Although he was promoted to full professor for his second year at Bryn Mawr, and he and Ellen moved into a house of their own, Wilson began to seek another job, preferably at Princeton. His initial salary of $1200 was raised to $1800 for the second year, and he tried earnestly to follow his father's advice: "Hasten slowly. A year or so at Bryn Mawr will be nothing lost" (Baker I, 260). During his first year he wrote "Reponsible Government Under the Constitution," which was published in the *Atlantic Monthly* for April 1886 and was essentially an expansion and further development of ideas in *Congressional Government*. In March 1886 he addressed the Princeton alumni, an earnest, serious attempt that was essentially unsuccessful at a gathering devoted largely to having a good time. Later that spring he went to Washington, hoping to find a place in the Department of State. Unsuccessful and discouraged, he resigned himself to remaining at Bryn Mawr; he was only temporarily elevated by the birth of his first daughter, Margaret, on April 16, in Georgia.

While his wife and new child gained strength in Georgia, Wilson visited Boston, conferring with the editors of the *Atlantic* and with his publishers, Houghton Mifflin. Stimulated, he began to plan his next work, a multivolume study of politics, statecraft, and government. The first part of this—what he called a "dull fact book," essentially a textbook—was what was to be published in 1889 as *The State: Elements of Historical and Practical Politics.* In order to carry on his research he began to learn German as well as to improve his French. Enthused by his new project, nevertheless he found himself limited by practicality. A projected study tour of Germany was delayed indefinitely while he sought means of adding to his income, chiefly by writing and lecturing.

I   *Political Essays*

His writing resulted in two essays published in 1887, "Of the Study of Politics," published in the *New Princeton Review* in March 1887, and "The Study of Administration," published in the *Political Science Quarterly* in June 1887. Both essays are essentially philosophic rather than practical in nature despite their titles. In the former, he insisted that "to know anything about government, you must *see it alive,*" a departure from the detachment that dominated *Congressional Government,* and in the latter he began to formulate ideas that stemmed from his concept of administration as a science.

It is this essay that provides the first suggestion that his ideas were beginning to move away from the preoccupation with Congress and with the parliamentary system that had dominated his thinking through the writing of *Congressional Government.* Somewhat later than the beginning of change suggested by Walter Lippmann in his introduction to *Congressional Government,*[2] nevertheless these new ideas point toward increasing centralization of executive power as he comments upon the growth of governmental structures, the interrelationships of government and big business, and the inevitable growth of extranational government. The evidence suggests that here, at Bryn Mawr, the unhappy young professor had begun to lay the foundations for what would become, a quarter of a century later, Wilson's New Freedom and, even later, his vision of world order.

The evidence suggests, too, that Wilson spent a good deal of time polishing the prose of these essays, determined to make them not only literary and hence "beautiful to read," but, more importantly, to make them eloquent statements of position, and the result is apparent: both of them are a great deal more forceful and moving than the sometimes ponderous and clever prose of his earlier essays.

On August 28, 1887, the second Wilson daughter, Jessie Woodrow, was born, and that fall Wilson felt more futile than before. "Thirty-one years old and nothing done!" he commented hopelessly.

His teaching was demanding but unsatisfying, research facilities were virtually nonexistent, and the intellectual life at Bryn Mawr was limited. Although many of his women students later commented on his brilliance as a lecturer during these years, nevertheless his inability to relax was evident to them. Even in a volunteer current-events discussion class, held every two weeks, "it was clear that Mr. Wilson preferred to carry on the main discussion himself" (Baker I, 291). In a letter to his wife on October 4, 1887, he defined his own position:

> I don't see how a literary life can be built upon foundations of under-graduate instruction. That instruction compels you to live with the commonplaces, the A.B.C. of every subject and to dwell upon these with an emphasis and an invention altogether disproportioned to their intrinsic weight and importance—it keeps you on the dusty, century-travelled highroads of every subject, from which you get no outlooks except those that are catalogued and vulgarized in every guide-book. You get weary of the plodding and yet you get habituated to it, more and more so. What *is* a fellow to do? How is he to earn bread and at the same time find leisure for thoughts detached from the earning of bread? (Baker I, 292–93)

Nevertheless Wilson continued to find the time if not leisure for other work, writing a chapter, "Taxation and Appropriation," for a book by his friend Albert Shaw, and continuing to work on *The State*. Although early in the fall of 1887 he began to fear a breakdown in health if he remained another year at Bryn Mawr, he revived later that fall by seeking a possible appointment as Assistant Secretary of State, but nothing came of his hopes. When his mother died in April 1888, he was shattered. "My mother was a mother to me in the fullest, sweetest sense of the word, and her loss has left me with a sad, oppressive sense of having suddenly *lost my youth*" (Baker I, 295), he wrote a month later, as his spirits began to rise.

Later that summer the opportunity came to move to Wesleyan University. "I have for a long time been hungry for a class of *men*" (Baker I, 295), he wrote in delight as he worked with vigor on *The State*. That fall he became professor of History and Political Economy at Wesleyan. Wilson began with fervor to take up where he had left off at Johns Hopkins: he organized a Wesleyan House of Commons, helped coach the football team, and began a series of twenty-five lectures at Johns Hopkins for which he was to receive the sum of $500. Apparently he enjoyed his two years at Wesleyan.

In September 1888 Wilson published his first "literary" essay, "An

Old Master," in the *New Princetonian*. Both practical and philosophical in nature, the essay discussed the improvement of college lecturing, a teaching technique in which Wilson excelled, largely, as he made clear in the essay, because of the care with which he organized, developed, and wrote lectures. Intensely critical of his own work, on February 13, 1889, he wrote from Johns Hopkins to his wife:

> I have gotten the impression, somehow (perhaps through my imagination), that my two lectures, so far delivered, have fallen rather flat, and I feel a whit discouraged: but the attention of the class must, shall, be conquered before I get through with them. It's my sensibilities, rather than my courage, that are wounded. To tell the truth, my second lecture was poor,—thrown together, undigested, ill-arranged, inorganic: I can do better. . . . (Baker I, 301)

II The State

In the fall of 1889 *The State* was published. Wilson described it as "a fact book, . . . always a plebeian among books," but, he wrote, "a great deal has gone out of me into it, none the less. . . ." His most carefully researched work, it was also the first of its kind, a fact of which he was quite proud. Essentially it ranges widely in its examination of the development of government. At the same time it provides a good deal of insight into Wilson's concept of the nature of the state, its functions, and its objectives.

The State may be divided into two parts. The first, chapters I through XII, discusses the developing forms of government, ranging from the earliest forms through evolution and revolution to modern states, essentially those of western Europe as well as that of the United States. This, of course, is the major part of the book, but the most revealing is that section composed of chapters XIII through XVI, which are essentially philosophical and interpretive; in them Wilson attempts a massive synthesis.

Each of the first group of chapters is based on the best, newest scholarship in history, government, and political science, and Wilson brought them up to date several times, particularly in the editions of 1898 and 1911. His major source, he acknowledges, is *Handbuch des oeffentlichen Rechts der Gegenwort*, the massive series of monographs on modern governments, edited by Professor Heinrich Marquardsen of the University of Erlangen. The series provides an example of much of the best and some of the worst of the German scholarship that Wilson greatly admired during his academic career.

Wilson's first chapter in *The State*, the most speculative, deals with the earliest forms of government, tracing "how, at last, kinsmen became fellow citizens." From this point he examines the governments of Greece and Rome and of the European Middle Ages, emphasizing particularly the effect of Roman law upon gradually emerging national states. From these evolve the variety of governments of western Europe and the United States: the contrasting unitary governments of France and Great Britain; the federal empire of Germany; the dual monarchies of Austria-Hungary and Sweden-Norway; the federal republics of Switzerland and the United States. These are examined in comparative, evolutionary, and constitutional evaluations that define clearly and at the same time accept completely the implications of Darwinism for the study of society.

His conclusions accept this essentially Darwinian point of view, especially in his discussion of the functions of government, which, Wilson asserts, are determined by circumstance and experience. In the context of governmental functions he sees a basic similarity in diversity:

One may justly conclude, not indeed that the restraints which modern states put upon themselves are of little consequence, or that altered political conceptions are not of the greatest moment in determining important questions of government and even the whole advance of the race; but that it is rather by gaining practical wisdom, rather than by long processes of historical experience, that states modify their practices. New theories are subsequent to new experiences.[3]

In his discussion of "The Objects of Government" Wilson moves beyond synthesis to define not merely what is, but also what should be, in the process giving not only insight into Wilson as essentially a Jeffersonian, but also providing glimpses of the Wilson who was to appear dramatically on the American political stage two decades later. In the main it is clear that Wilson has become a Cleveland Democrat, seeking a new balance between the Democratic values of a pre–Civil War society and a dynamic, dangerous industrial reality:

What part shall government play in the affairs of society?—that is the question which has been the gauge of controversial battle. Stated in another way, it is the very question which I postponed when discussing the functions of government. "*What,*" namely, "*ought the functions of government to be?*" On the one hand there are extremists who cry constantly to government, "Hands off," "*laissez fiare,*" "*laissez passer*"! who look upon every act of government which is not merely an act of police with jealousy, who regard government as necessary, but as a necessary evil, and who would have government hold back from everything which could by any possibility be accomplished by individual initiative and endeavor. On the other hand, there are those who, with equal extremeness of view in the opposite direction, would have society lean fondly upon government for guidance and assistance in every power and beneficence caught in the pages of ancient or mediaeval historian or by some dream of co-operative endeavor cunningly imagined by the great fathers of Socialism, believe that the state can be made a wise foster-mother to every member of the family politic. Between these two extremes, again, there are all grades, all shades and colors, all degrees of enmity or of partiality to state action.[4]

The origins of this point of view, seeking a clear definition of an ideal relationship between government and the governed, are evident in the evolving Democratic party as it moved from the anti-Federalist rejection of central power to the more balanced view of the Jacksonians, who looked to government for wanted help but at the same time regarded it with skeptical suspicion. It is this middle ground, largely dominated in the 1880s and early 1890s by the pre-Bryan party of Grover Cleveland, that, Wilson was convinced, was the ground government must occupy:

But there is a middle ground. The schemes which Socialists have proposed society assuredly cannot accept and no scheme which involves the complete control of the individual by government can be devised which differs from theirs very much for the better. A truer doctrine must be found, which gives wide freedom to the individual for his self-development and yet guards that freedom against the competition that kills, and reduces the antagonism between self-development and social development to a minimum. And such a doctrine can be formulated, surely, without too great vagueness.[5]

Here, it is evident, Wilson is not looking to the past, nor, as some critics have observed, is he revealing an essential conservatism that had presumably dominated his thinking during his thirties. Rather, it is quite clear that here, twenty years before the impact of Louis Brandeis and William Jennings Bryan on Wilson's thinking, the relationships to which some critics attribute much of Wilson's progressivism, Wilson is moving toward the *New Freedom*. "The end of government is," he insists, ". . . to accomplish the ends of organized society"; consequently, "to society alone can the power of dominating combinations belong: and society cannot suffer any of its members to enjoy such a power for their own private gain independently of its own strict regulation or oversight."[6] Thus, Wilson's concept of the proper province of government is that of a regulatory force actively intervening in what is properly the public sector for the good of society:

> There are some things outside the field of natural monopolies in which individual action cannot secure equalization of the conditions of competition. . . . By forbidding child labor, by supervising the sanitary conditions of factories, by limiting the employment of women in occupations hurtful to their health, by instituting official tests of the purity or the quality of goods sold, by limiting the hours of labor in certain trades, by a hundred and one limitations of the power of unscrupulous or heartless men to out-do the scrupulous and merciful in trade or industry, government has assisted equity. . . . In scores of such cases government has intervened and will intervene; but by way, not of interference, by way, rather, of making competition equal. . . . It is in this way that society protects itself against permanent injury and deterioration, and secures healthful equality of opportunity for self-development.[7]

This is hardly the rejection of a governmental role in the regulation of business, but rather the advocation of governmental activity for the well-being of society as a whole. Government should never dominate society, he warned, because society by its very nature is greater and vastly more important than government. Therefore, he makes clear a vital distinction between interference in the affairs of society—an intrusion never warranted—and a proper activity "in the best interests of the social organism." This is essentially the position held by Progressives and Bryan Democrats of the *fin de siècle* and of a resurgent, Wilson-led Democratic party in 1912.

The State is thus an important work for Wilson not only because it became important in his academic career, but because it gave him the opportunity to begin to organize his thinking on the proper role of government. Not merely a "book of facts," his father's comment, "Woodrow, couldn't you have put more juice in it?" is not entirely justified. *The State* is packed, but it is informative, provocative, carefully organized, and logical—all elements necessary for the successful teacher-scholar. At the same time it is a dramatic book, taking for its substance the sweep of the evolution of Western society, certainly man's most complex creation. And in *The State* Wilson gives order, form, and direction to that panorama. The result is both visionary and dramatic, and it makes possible for Wilson a first tentative bridge between past and future.

CHAPTER 5

The Senior Professor

THE publication of *The State* was the major accomplishment of Wilson's two happy, productive years at Wesleyan. He accepted the invitation of Professor Albert Bushnell Hart of Harvard to write the third and final volume of the "Epochs of American History" series, edited by Hart, which was published in 1893 as *Division and Reunion, 1829–1889*. During his last year at Wesleyan he became profoundly disappointed with political developments as Benjamin Harrison defeated Cleveland: "What is to be the *policy* of such an administration?" he wondered. "I don't know whether to laugh or rage." He resolutely refused to attend the inauguration.

Nevertheless, political theory and thinking dominated his two years at Wesleyan. In the March 1889 issue of the *Political Science Quarterly* he provided an incisive critical review of James Bryce's *American Commonwealth*, and in the *Atlantic Monthly* for November 1889 he attempted a definition of the "Character of Democracy in the United States." Wilson based his definition upon an organic concept of democracy that stems directly from the Darwinian vision of *The State*:

Democracy is of course wrongly conceived when treated as merely a body of doctrine, or as simply a form of government. It is a stage of development. It is not created by aspirations or by new faith: it is built up by slow habit. Its process is experience, its basis old want, its meaning national organic unity and effectual life. It comes, like manhood, as the fruit of youth: immature peoples cannot have it, and the maturity to which it is vouchsafed is the maturity of freedom and self-control, and no other. It is conduct, and its only stable foundation is character. America has democracy because she is free; she is not free because she has democracy. . . . (Baker-Dodd I, I, 176–77)

In this curious blend of traditional morality and inexorable evolution, Wilson approaches Carl Becker's concept of democracy in *Every Man His Own Historian*, but without Becker's pessimism. In a series

56

of lectures at Brown University that November, Wilson explored, again in terms reminiscent of *The State*, the topic "State and Social Reforms," and advocated a rejection of the extremes and a search for the middle but active way.

I *The Return to Princeton*

Nevertheless, in spite of his active happiness at Wesleyan, when the opportunity presented itself to join the Princeton faculty as professor of Jurisprudence and Politics in the fall of 1890, Wilson did not hesitate, and, as Ray Stannard Baker has pointed out, his twelve years as a member of the Princeton faculty were among the most crucial of his public and professional career.

During these years Wilson became a major figure in American higher education as his career advanced: he continued his lectures at Johns Hopkins; he lectured regularly at the New York School of Law; he made a major address at the Chicago World's Fair in 1893; he became popular as a speaker at Princeton alumni gatherings; and at the same time he increased his reputation as a teacher-scholar. During these years he was offered the presidency of seven universities: Illinois, Virginia, Alabama, Washington and Lee, Nebraska, Minnesota, and finally, in 1902, Princeton.

The Princeton to which Wilson returned in 1890 was still the College of New Jersey; it had not yet begun its transition to Princeton University (the name was not changed until 1896, at the Princeton sesquicentennial celebration, at which Wilson was the chief speaker). During the early years of his return Wilson began gradually to formulate the ideas that would provide the basis of his attempts at reform as university president. Thus, in his address at the Chicago World's Fair, Wilson answered with a strong affirmative his topical question, "Should an Antecedent Liberal Education Be Required of Students in Law, Medicine and Theology?" and he emphasized the same point in an address before the American Bar Association and in an article, "Legal Education of Undergraduates," in the *Forum*, edited by Walter Hines Page. In a later article, he expanded his idea to include a social duty: "It is the object of learning, not only to satisfy the curiosity and perfect the spirits of individual men, but also to advance civilization. . . ."[1]

Consequently, to Wilson, the University, if it is to serve its purpose, must seek a new synthesis, a common educational foundation. In defining the means whereby this foundation might be provided, he advocated a system long in use in English universities, and which he would make a major policy goal as president: "A considerable number of young tutors, serving their novitiate for full university appointments, might easily enough effect an organization of the men that would secure the [necessary] readings."[2]

Finally, at the sesquicentennial address on October 21, 1896, Wilson began to make clear his concept of the ideal university. His talk was called "Princeton in the Nation's Service"; published in the *Forum* and widely quoted, it was a major statement of purpose and philosophy.

In this speech Wilson developed his concept of the role of the university as "a school of duty," in which professors must not forget that "they are training citizens as well as drilling pupils." The past, Wilson pointed out in great detail, had been merely prefatory to Princeton's future, although it, too, had been a record of outstanding contributions. Consequently, his new university would be firmly rooted in the studies and techniques that had made that record possible:

> Can anyone wonder, then, that I ask for the old drill, the old memory of times gone by, the old schooling in precedent and tradition, the old keeping of faith with the past, as a preparation for leadership in days of social change? We have not given science too big a place in our education; but we have made a perilous mistake in giving it too great a preponderance in method in every other branch of study. We must make the humanities human again; must recall what manner of men we are; must turn back once more to the region of practicable ideals.
>
> Of course, when all is said, it is not learning but the spirit of service that will give a college place in the public annals of the nation. It is indispensable, it seems to me, if it is to do its right service, that the air of affairs should be admitted to all its classrooms.· . . . We dare not keep aloof and closet ourselves when a nation comes to its maturity. The days of glad expansion are gone, our life grows tense and difficult; our resource for the future lies in careful thought, providence, and a wise economy; and the school must be that of the nation.
>
> I have had sight of the perfect place of learning in my thought: a free place, and a various, where no man could be and not know with how great a destiny knowledge had come into the world—. . . . Who shall show our way to this place? (Baker-Dodd I, I, 70–71)

Increasingly prominent Princetonians, particularly among the alumni, were convinced that Woodrow Wilson was the man who would lead the university into its rightful place at the center of the nation's affairs. But, although there is evidence to suggest that Wilson anticipated his election to Princeton's presidency during those years, he devoted much attention to the political affairs of the nation, and he did a great deal of writing. Often those fields overlapped, particularly in two essays, "Mr. Cleveland's Cabinet" in *Review of Reviews* for April 1893, and "Mr. Cleveland as President" in the *Atlantic Monthly* for March 1897, which was then edited by his friend Walter Hines Page.

Wilson's attention was focused upon public affairs during those years not only because of his admiration for Grover Cleveland, a major factor in his changing view of the Presidency, but because those were times that demanded a great deal of attention. As Wilson made clear in his sesquicentennial address, he was well aware of the fact that America's frontier had closed, and with that closing, the nation's youth and freedom of movement had passed. The new America was increasingly an industrial mass society that limited individual social mobility.

In the last years of the 1880s Wilson was not only acutely aware of President Cleveland's accession to the Presidency as the first Democrat since Buchanan, but he was aware too of industrial crisis: the founding of the American Federation of Labor in 1886; the great railway strikes of 1886–1887; the Haymarket Square Riot in 1886; the establishment of the Interstate Commerce Commission; the accession of another of the mediocre Civil War generals, Benjamin Harrison, to the Presidency; the Sherman Anti-Trust Act of 1890; the abominable McKinley Tariff of 1890; continued labor trouble at Homestead, Pennsylvania, at Pullman, Illinois, and elsewhere; Coxey's army; the reelection of Mr. Cleveland; the spread of depression and panic; and then, gradually, the emergence of McKinley and the planting of the seeds of imperialism and populism, the former to flourish while the latter brought William Jennings Bryan (whom Wilson did not support for the Presidency in 1896) dramatically to national prominence.

In both of his assessments of Cleveland and his performance, Wilson was satisfied. Cleveland moved with vigor and forthrightness in a course usually but not always conservative. His eloquent conclusion to the second essay was perhaps responsible for the close relationship between the two when Cleveland became a trustee of Princeton. At the same time it suggests a concept of the Presidency greatly changed since the publication of *Congressional Government* only a few years before:

We need not pretend to know what history shall say of Mr. Cleveland; we need not pretend that we can draw any common judgment of the man from the confused cries that now ring everywhere from friend and foe. We only know that he has played a great part; that his greatness is authenticated by the passion of love and hatred he has stirred up; that no such great personality has appeared in our politics since Lincoln; and that, whether greater or less, his personality is his own, unique in all the varied history of our government. He has made policies and altered parties after the fashion of an earlier age in our history, and the men who assess his fame in the future will be no partisans, but men who love candor, courage, honesty, strength, unshaken capacity, and high purpose such as his. (Baker-Dodd I, I, 308–309)

Such an endorsement is not only a passionate political and personal endorsement, but it is at the same time an eloquent and practical tribute to a political organization and party, indebting Democratic partisans in a manner that ultimately permitted Wilson to assume his two presidencies.

During these years of the 1890s, Wilson was not only most productive of literature and ideas, but he began once more to experience illness that at times threatened to incapacitate him. In 1896 and 1899 he recuperated in Europe, in at least one instance practicing writing with his left hand because his right hand was threatened with paralysis. Nevertheless, during those years he published in addition to his essays a number of important critical reviews of major works by others and four books of his own, and he completed much of the work for his five-volume *History of the American People*, published in 1902.

II   Division and Reunion

The first of his books during his Princeton tenure was *Division and Reunion, 1829–1889*. Published in 1893, it has unfortunately been neglected by Wilson's biographers and critics, largely because it is part of a three-volume history of American politics that is, as Wilson called it in his preface, "a rapid synopsis—as rapid as possible—of the larger features of public affairs in the crowded space of sixty years that stretches from the election of Andrew Jackson to the end of the first century of the Constitution." Just as *The State* is much more revealing than Wilson's description suggests, the same thing may be said of *Division and Reunion*.

The two most obvious features of the book are its remarkable objectivity—although on several occasions Wilson's bias, particularly toward Democratic conservatism, does become obvious—and its remarkably readable style. In writing to Albert Bushnell Hart, after accepting the contract to write the book, he had been confident of his objectivity:

Your confidence in my impartiality I greatly value—and shall hope to deserve. Though born in the South and bred in its sympathies, I am not of Southern-born parents. My father was born in Ohio, my mother in England. Ever since I have had independent judgments of my own I have been a Federalist (!) It is this mixture of elements in me—full identification with the South, non-Southern blood, and Federalist principles—that makes me hope that a detachment of my affectionate, reminiscent sympathies from my historical judgments is not beyond hoping for. (Baker I, 307)

The book is, as Wilson points out, deliberately out of balance. The section that deals with the twelve years between Jackson's accession to the Presidency and the capture of that office by the Whigs in 1841 is considerably longer in proportion than those that deal with the growth of the slavery crisis, secession and civil war, and "Rehabilitation of the Union." He uses this proportion because, as he rightly pointed out from his perspective of the last decade of the nineteenth century, the Jacksonian era marked the conclusion of the period of consolidation that had begun in the Revolution and the beginning of the growth of a new democratic social and political ideal.

The sixty years covered by the volume were not only the most complex and tragic in American history, but at the time of Wilson's writing and even yet they have been among the most difficult to assess objectively and to treat with the dispatch which the scope of the volume demanded, two problems of which Wilson was well aware: "It was of course a period of misunderstanding and of passion; and I cannot claim to have judged rightly in all cases as between parties. I can claim, however, impartiality of judgment; for impartiality is a matter of the heart, and I know with what disposition I have written.[3]

To a great extent the same concept of organic growth and orderly evolution that characterized the treatment of political change in *The State* provides the philosophical foundation of this volume, but the much greater detail in treatment often accelerates the movement of events. Thus, the twelve years of Jacksonian domination provide the background for a rapid growth of Jackson's political principles—the speedy expansion of the franchise to more and more men (of which Wilson obviously approved—up to a point), the massive and successful assault on the Bank of the United States and the subsequent transfer of economic power to public hands (both of which Wilson apparently disapproved—up to a point), the dynamic, often brawling personal approach to political action (which Wilson obviously disliked). One can almost hear, in Wilson's summary of the period, an echo of Emerson's assertion that, while the Democrats had the best policies, the Whigs had the best men.

Wilson's treatment of the intensification of the slavery crisis, the attempts to denationalize the issue and to compromise it away, and the steady erosion of American institutions moves with the solemn inevitability of Greek tragedy as good will, statesmanship, and ultimately men themselves meet the crisis and fail to resolve it. Wilson's understanding of the Southern position is evident, as is his attempt to withhold the judgment that historical assessment of the period demands, but at the same time it is evident that to Wilson the slavery issue was ultimately a moral rather than a legal or political problem, and in much the same terms that Lincoln expressed in his second inaugural address, Wilson makes clear his conviction that it had to be resolved on moral terms. Perhaps here, in an academic work written in a time of relative ease and happiness, Wilson had begun to lay the foundations for his view of the great events of 1917, 1918, and 1919.

Much of Wilson's interpretation of the post–Civil War years, and particularly of the 1880s, is economic in nature, and it is here, more than in any other section of the book, that his conservative orientation is evident. Thus as the Greenbackers and Populists emerged in the political wars between East and West, country and city, Wilson made clear his position: "Gold was regarded, therefore by that large class of persons who cannot comprehend monetary questions as 'dear' money, and the coinage of silver was demanded, in order that the country might have an abundance of 'cheap' money. . . ."[4] Nevertheless, this attitude is tempered not only by a natural sympathy but also by a reflection of his innate morality: much of the blame for the intensification of the country's financial problem is the fault of "the 'monied interest' of the East," who threaten ". . . a government of the country from Wall Street. . . ."[5]

Wilson's sympathy for Cleveland's vigorous action after so much Presidential inaction is equally evident, suggesting that the interpretation of the American governmental system that provided the substance of *Congressional Government* had become considerably modified by the end of the first Cleveland administration.

Wilson ends, firmly aware of the problems yet facing the nation, with a curious blend of uncertainty and certainty, conservatism and a liberalism based on morality. Immigration had become a threat rather than an asset, yet at its heart was the moral injustice and prejudice that brought about the Chinese Exclusion Act; natural resources and industrialism promise a new era of freedom and fulfillment; yet "self-indulgence and fashion displayed and distorted themselves as never before in the sober republic,"[6] and, as the nation moved confidently into its second century,

new troubles came, hot conflicts between capital and labor; but the new troubles bred new thinkers, and the intellectual life of the nation was but the more deeply stirred. As the equilibrium of parties tempered political action, so the presence of new problems quickened sober thought, disposed the nation to careful debate of its future. The century ended with a new sense of preparation, a new seriousness, and a new hope.[7]

Neither imperialism nor progressivism shadowed Wilson's conclusions, although both were to become major forces in the life of the nation before the end of the decade and of the nineteenth century. The tone of the book, combined with the literate ease of Wilson's prose, makes evident a sense of purpose and of intelligent hope that anticipates further and continuous growth, expansion, and political and social development. Wilson's conviction that the elimination of the moral cancer of slavery had made possible a new era of American evolution toward the social perfection that is its birthright is perhaps the most eloquent section of the book. And, however one may quarrel with Wilson's interpretations and conclusions, or even facts omitted or altered, as did critics North and South, academic and general, the book is still, more than three quarters of a century later, a pleasure to read and an example of how history should be written but rarely is. Wilson's preoccupation with style, with the aesthetic as well as functional dimension of language, is nowhere more evident or more successful than in this deceptively simple, often-over looked work.

III   An Old Master and Other Political Essays

Wilson followed *Division and Reunion* with *An Old Master and Other Political Essays*, also published in 1893. A collection of essays that Wilson had written during the previous ten years or so, they are essentially philosophical rather than historical, giving, perhaps, substance, as does some of the criticism directed at *Division and Reunion* by his fellow historians, to the argument that his prime consideration was stylistic and interpretive rather than factual. As *An Old Master and Other Political Essays* was being prepared for the press, he wrote to Caleb Thomas Winchester that

the tribe I professionally belong to (historians, economists, jurists—what not!) are desperately dull fellows. They have no more *literature* in them than an ass has of beauty. They don't know anything, because they know only *one* thing; and I am terribly afraid of growing like them. I am not only not a scholar, but I don't want to be one. . . .[8]

As Wilson suggests in this letter, his major interests, more obvious in his shorter works, primarily essays, than in his longer, more academic works, are intellectual and stylistic rather than conventionally scholarly. The essays in this first collection, as in his later collection, *Mere Literature and Other Essays* (1896), are illustrative of these interests. The first, "An Old Master," the title essay of the volume, is, however, commentary on one of Wilson's long-standing interests: the art of lecturing, a topic not only usually ignored by both his contemporary academics and his successors, but denigrated by those few—usually dedicated members of College of Education faculties—who do mention it.

Wilson was not only a gifted and extremely popular lecturer, enjoyed by his students as well as the public at large, but he was one of the few who had devoted much time and thought to the process. Not only was the substance of his lectures carefully prepared—his lecture notes are among the most interesting of his remaining manuscripts—but the presentation of them was also the subject of thought, preparation, and even, at times, careful rehearsal.

For the substance of the essay, Wilson focuses upon the academic career of Adam Smith, who, Wilson asserts, owed his advancement in the intellectual world to his success as a lecturer in the university world:

It appears clear that his success was due to two things: the broad outlook of his treatment and the fine art of his style. His chair was Moral Philosophy; and "moral philosophy" seems to have been the most inclusive of general terms in the university usage of Scotland at that day, and, indeed, for many years afterwards. . . . Adam Smith, in Glasgow, could draw within the big family of this large-hearted philosophy not only the science of mental phenomena, but also the whole of the history and organization of society. . . .[9]

Such a man seeks for himself, in typical fashion of the eighteenth century of which he was intrinsically a part, the mastery of all knowledge, and beyond that, the role of philosopher who seeks to synthesize, to extract from the mass of raw information provided by himself and others the natural laws that govern the affairs of men and the functioning of the universe of which they are a part. This was the role Smith chose for himself as a university lecturer[10] and ultimately in his writing *The Wealth of Nations*, a work whose "conclusions are, first of all, philosophical, only secondarily practical. . . .[11] he was no specialist, except *in the relations of things.*"[12]

Perhaps reflective of some of the academic criticism directed at some of his works, particularly *Division and Reunion*, Wilson defines his own role as lecturer-writer at the same time that he defines that of Adam Smith:

Of course, spreading his topics far and wide in the domain of history and philosophy, he was at many points superficial. He took most of his materials at second-hand; and it has been said that he borrowed many of his ideas from the French. But no matter who mined the gold, he minted it. . . . Adam Smith was doubtless indebted to the Physiocrats, but all the world is indebted to Adam Smith. . . .[13]

Wilson concludes the essay with a projection into his academic present, and, in tones reminiscent of the eighteenth century out of which Smith came, Wilson proclaims the role of one who, like Jefferson's natural aristocrats, rises above his contemporaries to teach them, or who, in Emerson's terms, becomes their representative man. For Wilson, the great teacher is not unlike the great political leaders he continued to admire: "Education and the world of thought need men who, like this man, will dare to know a multitude of things. Without them and their bold synthetic methods, all knowledge and all thought would fall apart into a weak analysis. Their minds do not lack in thoroughness; their thoroughness simply lacks in minuteness. . . ."[14]

More than this, however, such a man is also an artist:

For him things stand out in picturesque relations; their great outlines fit into each other; the touch of his treatment is necessarily broad and strong. The same informing influence of artistic conception and combination gives to his style its luminous and yet transparent qualities . . . such men must write *literature,* or nothing. . . . By reason of the very strength of their humanity, they are enabled to say things long waiting to be said, in such a way that all men may receive them. . . . They hold commissions from the King of Speech. . . .[15]

In the following essays in the collection, Wilson demonstrates this concept of the teacher-philosopher-artist in action. In "The Study of Politics," therefore, Wilson insists that there is a continuum between practical politics and political philosophy, and he who would master the latter must not ignore the former: "If politics were to be studied as a great department of human conduct, not to be understood by a scholar who is not also a man of the world, its literature might be made as imperishable as that of the imagination. There might then enter into it that which is immortal. . . ."[16]

"Political Sovereignty," "Character of Democracy in the United States," and "Government Under the Constitution," the last three essays in the collection, further illustrate Wilson's search for the philosophical-artistic synthesis. Thus, "the conception of political sovereignty is one of those interesting portions of doctrine which belong in common to several distinct branches of study"; the concept is essentially critical and philosophic, but our scholars too often stop short of attempting to make the syntheses that Wilson constructs of the concepts of constitutions and law-making bodies.

In his definition of the nature of democracy in America Wilson again asserts the role of "dominant minds," selected by the electorate, and that leadership must then act, for "progress is motion, government is action. The waters of democracy are useless in their reservoirs unless they may be used to drive the wheels of policy and administration."[17] This leadership, he asserts, in terms reminiscent of *Congressional Government,* must inevitably be legislative if we are to remain at once a democracy and a nation that remains such by obeying leaders.

"The Constitution" looks back to *Congressional Government* and forward to *Constitutional Government in the United States,* which was to draw heavily on changing political circumstances, Wilson's increased political knowledge, and his research for courses and lectures, and which was ultimately published in 1909. In the essay Wilson asserts that the program for the nation that is defined in the Constitution has not been carried out and that Congress has begun to approach the level of a mass meeting rather than a deliberative legislative body. Legislation has become haphazard, largely the result of pressures from varied, often competing sources; what is needed are programs, plans, and logical platforms, all sanctioned by the popular voice, the voice of the people who have delegated authority to their representatives.

As a whole the volume is a clear illustration of Wilson's theory of the intellectual-artistic synthesis. Each of the essays is not only well written and persuasive, but the book is a complete political statement and an illustration of his philosophy of communication. There is much opportunity to quarrel with Wilson's approach and to reject his conclusions, largely because he sweeps broadly in generalizations that are impressive but unsupported, and in most cases evidence is nothing more than assertion. But the essays read well, they are persuasive, and they carry with them the air of authority, perhaps of being, as Wilson's eighteenth-century mentors would insist, self-evident truths within the context of the search for a synthesis that interprets men and their political institutions.

During the several years following the publication of *An Old Master and Other Essays*, Wilson continued to write prolifically, including the essays that he was to collect in *Mere Literature and Other Essays*, a variety of reviews and review essays, and his next historical study, *George Washington*. Written first as a series of articles at the instigation of Henry M. Alden, editor of *Harper's Magazine*, Wilson's biography of Washington was well received, and its publication in 1896 led to the first "Wilson Dinner," held by thirty members of his Princeton class of 1879, and which was undoubtedly influential in the later election of Wilson to Princeton's presidency in 1902.

Before its book publication, however, Wilson's *George Washington* was published in serial form in *Harper's Magazine*. The first essay, "In Washington's Day," appeared in January 1896. "Colonel Washington" appeared in March; "At Home in Virginia," in May; "General Washington," in July; "First in Peace," in September; and "The First President of the United States," in November. Book publication followed, with the articles divided into ten chapters but with otherwise minor revisions.

While the book was in press, near the end of May 1896, it appears that Wilson suffered a slight stroke, which caused some pain and impairment of functioning in his right hand. Nevertheless, on May 30 he sailed for Europe. The journey was primarily a pilgrimage to the places associated with the ancestry of his ideas, his culture, and his admiration as well as that of his family. He returned to New York on September 7, somewhat recovered from the apparent stroke, and by the following March he had recovered completely. On the trip he did some work on the manuscript for *Mere Literature and Other Essays*, in June sending to his wife a copy of his proposed dedication to her brother, Stockton Axson.

Upon his return he prepared for his important speech "Princeton in the Nation's Service," to be given on October 21 at the university's sesquicentennial, and he read proofs of his two forthcoming books. The initial reception of *George Washington* in both article and book form was good, as was the earlier reception of *Mere Literature and Other Essays*, which was to remain one of Wilson's own favorites among his works, and the one, he insisted, that gave him the most pleasure to write and to remember.

IV   Mere Literature and Other Essays

Mere Literature and Other Essays was published in November 1896, a month before *George Washington*. Like *An Old Master and Other Essays*, it is a collection of eight essays that had, with one exception, been published earlier in the *Atlantic Monthly*, *Century Magazine*, or the *Forum*. Of this collection, the title essay is that which Wilson felt most deeply and wrote most passionately. Published in the *Atlantic Monthly* for December 1893, it is an attack on the so-called "scientific" approach to literary study, emphasizing textual criticism and philology, and at the time most popular at Wilson's own graduate alma mater, Johns Hopkins. Essentially the essay is an insistence rather than a mere plea that literature be studied for its own sake as a medium by which the values of Western civilization are transmitted and, at the same time, from which aesthetic pleasures may be derived from the style of the work. Apparently Wilson's brother-in-law and friend, Stockton Axson, to whom the volume was dedicated, had earlier told Wilson that James Wilson Bright, Johns Hopkins's distinguished philologist, had referred to a work as "mere literature." Later, when the Johns Hopkins English department did not appoint Wilson's friend Caleb Thomas Winchester of Wesleyan to the Donovan Chair of English Literature, Wilson apparently decided that an attack was in order before the situation at Hopkins became hopeless. He apparently wrote the essay in the spring of 1893.[18] Wilson begins the essay with an ironic definition:

A singular phrase, this, "mere literature," the irreverent invention of a scientific age. Literature, we know, but "mere literature"? We are not to read it as if it meant *sheer* literature, literature in the essence, stripped of all accidental or ephemeral elements, and left with nothing but its immortal charm and power. "Mere literature" is a serious sneer, conceived in all honesty by the scientific mind, which despises things which do not fall within the categories of demonstrable knowledge. It means *nothing but literature*, as who should say, "mere talk," "mere fabrication," "mere pastime." The scientist, with his head comfortably and excusably full of knowable things, takes nothing seriously and with his hat off except human knowledge. The creations of the human spirit are, from his point of view, incalculable vagaries, irresponsible phenomena, to be regarded only as play, and, for the mind's good, only as recreation,—to be used to while away the tedium of a railway journey, or to amuse a period of rest or convalescence; mere byplay, mere make-believe.[19]

The source and result of this denigration of what is to Wilson the central human creation, is the same: the exclusion of taste, judgment, or general interest from a field taken over for definition and examination by a small band of scholars who consequently "create Philistia, that country in which they speake of 'mere literature.' I suppose that in Nirvana one would speak in like wise of 'mere life.' "[20] These are the people, Wilson asserts, who speak of a work as written in "an 'admirable spirited style.' By this I take them to mean that it is grammatical, orderly, and full of strong adjectives."[21] Such a reaction is, in Wilson's view, only possible if one is completely ignorant of the nature or effects of literary style or incapable of reacting to the sheer power of literary greatness.

Essentially a great literature is, Wilson insists, the heir of a great tradition that, in the classic sense, "has a quality to move you, and you can never mistake it. And it has also a power to instruct you which is as effective as it is subtle, and which no research or systematic method can ever rival."[22]

The study of literature, then, Wilson asserts, concerns itself with these elements—with the study "not of forms or of differences, but of likenesses, likenesses of spirit and intent under whatever variety of method, running through all forms of speech like the same music along the chorus of various instruments."[23] The scientists, the products of the study of the concepts of evolution, study forms and differences, minutiae that obscure the intellectual, moral, and aesthetic unity that is Wilson's concept of essential literature. Unlike scientific methods, scholarship itself can become part of literature "by becoming part of the originating individuality of a master of thought . . . a master of . . . style. . . . Scholarship is material; it is not life." Literature, conversely, is to Wilson the essence of life, the source of whatever meaning and purpose life holds; that, he insists, is its purpose; "mere literature will keep us pure and keep us strong."[24]

Much of this essay is not merely an attack on scientific criticism, however; it is, more importantly, a statement of attitude, a revelation of Wilson's conviction that one might more properly speak of "mere scholarship," that which does not aspire to the permanent union of truth and beauty, particularity and universality. As early as 1891, he had written essentially the same thing to Horace Scudder:

> The fact of the matter is, that I am afraid to keep constantly intent upon my special topics of study. It is my creed that literary training and method are as essential to the production of good political science as to the production of good poetry or valid criticism. It is my practice, consequently, to try my hand, whenever I can, at various sorts of writing as unlike my professional tasks as possible. . . . (Baker II, 110)

Essentially, "Mere Literature" is both an expression of Wilson's literary ethic and at the same time one of those exercises in which he not only practiced and attempted to perfect his literary style but also in which he anticipated much of the criticism later directed at *George Washington* and *The History of the American People*. These works, Wilson was confident, were literary history rather than history alone. At the same time, they were in Ellen Axson Wilson's view the proper kind of work for the "man of letters" she was determined he would become (Baker II, 100).

The rest of the essays in the collection demonstrate Wilson's conviction that "scholarship cannot do without literature."[25] The two essays immediately following "Mere Literature," "The Author Himself" and "An Author's Company," are attempts to define the nature of the author, his purpose, his controlling ethic, and his values. Again, in essentially classic terms, Wilson decries the confusion that has beset authors who lose sight of their purpose: "Our novels have become sociological studies, our poems vehicles of criticism, our sermons political manifestos. We have confounded all processes in a common use, and do not know what we would be at."[26] If the author is to survive and to create, Wilson insists that he must redefine both his purpose and himself.

In the following two essays, "A Literary Politician" and "The Interpreter of English Liberty," Wilson provides illustrations of those authors, both English, whom he sees as those who produce what he calls essential literature. The first essay is devoted to an appreciation of Walter Bagehot, and the second, to Edmund Burke. Both essays are essentially biographical appreciations rather than critical essays, and in each Wilson sees the complete author, Burke perhaps the more nearly perfect than Bagehot, particularly when the two are compared:

> You would go to Burke, not to Bagehot, for inspiration in the infinite tasks of self-government; though you would, if you were wise, go to Bagehot rather than to Burke if you wished to realize just what were the practical daily conditions under which those tasks were to be worked out.
>
> Moreover, there is a deeper lack in Bagehot. He has no sympathy with the voiceless body of the people, with the "mass of unknown men." He conceives the work of government to be a work which is possible only to the instructed few. . . . He has not the stout fibre and the unquestioning faith in the right and capacity of inorganic majorities which make the democrat. . . .[27]

With this obvious movement away from the position of Bagehot, whom Ray Stannard Baker calls Wilson's "guide and exemplar," Wilson was moving in the direction of the democratic progressivism that characterized much of his presidency of Princeton, governorship of New Jersey, and first term as President of the United States. At the same time, in his essay on Burke he rediscovered the role of expediency in practical politics, a characteristic that Wilson sees as the essence of the popular appeal of political reform: "It is both better and easier to reform than to tear down and reconstruct. This is unquestionably the message of Englishmen to the world . . ."[28] just as ultimately it was the foundation of Wilson's concept of "The New Freedom," a reformation rather than a reconstruction of American social and political reality.

In "The Truth of the Matter" Wilson insists that "the historian needs an imagination quite as much as he needs scholarship,"[29] and in "A Calendar of Great Americans" and "The Course of American History," the last two essays in the volume, he demonstrates the relationship between the two. In the former essay, originally published in the *Forum,* February 1894, he first made a careful distinction between the nature of a "great American" and one who was simply a "great Englishman" who happened to be born in America. Furthermore, an added category was that of the "great provincial," one who was a great New Englander or great Southerner, and then there were "the authors of such thought as might have been native to any clime, like Asa Gray and Emerson; and the men of mixed breed, like Jefferson and Benton. . . ."[30]

Consequently, Wilson's definition of the "great American" elimi-
nates most of the founding fathers: Alexander Hamilton, because "he
believed in authority, and he had no faith in the aggregate wisdom of
masses of men . . . his ideas of government stuck fast in the old-world
politics, and his statesmanship was of Europe rather than America";[31]
James Madison, because he was "of the long line of English constitutional statesmen";[32] Thomas Jefferson, "because of the strain of
French philosophy that permeated and weakened all his thought;"[33]
to Wilson, in other words, the first generation of Americans were yet
largely transplanted Europeans.

Nevertheless, George Washington was "as thoroughly an American as Andrew Jackson or Abraham Lincoln,"[34] but John Adams and
John C. Calhoun were great provincials. The mainstream of great
Americans includes John Marshall and Daniel Webster among
"American constitutional statesmen"; and Benjamin Franklin, who
would "stand the final and characteristic test of Americanism: he
would unquestionably have made a successful frontiersman, capable
at once of wielding the axe and administering justice from the fallen
trunk."[35]

Among great Americans, those who fit this definition are Henry
Clay and Andrew Jackson, Robert E. Lee and Abraham Lincoln,
Ulysses S. Grant and Sam Houston, Patrick Henry and James Russell
Lowell, all of whom are "sound-hearted, hopeful, confident of the
validity of liberty, tenacious of the deeper principles of American
institutions, but with the old rashness schooled and sobered, and
instinct tempered by instruction. . . ."[36] With these characteristics,
essentially qualities of the national character, disseminated among all
Americans, Wilson proclaims, "then will come our great literature
and our greatest men."[37]

Wilson's final essay, essentially an address he had given before the
New Jersey Historical Society, is "The Course of American History,"
a brief rejection of the "Expansion of New England" theory of
American history so long propagated by the young men sent out by
Harvard and Yale to teach the nation. At the same time he rejects the
"Suppression of the South" theory propagated by young men from
Virginia and Georgia. The truth, Wilson insists, is that the course of
American history has been and will continue to be a national process,
made up of local and regional history that, combined, provides the
foundation of American greatness.

In the last two essays, as in the rest of the book, Wilson successfully
combines his subject matter with originality of idea and an easiness of

style to produce essays that coincide with his concept of literature. They are, in aggregate, stimulating if controversial; instructive if subjective; and, in general, essays that demand of the reader that he come to terms with them. Less scholarly than interpretive, nevertheless, the essays are indicative of Wilson's concern with the essence if not the substance of his discipline because, as he insisted at the end of "Mere Literature," "there is no science of literature. Literature in its essence is mere spirit, and you must experience it rather than analyze it too formally. It is the door to nature and to ourselves,"[38] rather than the recapitulation of the minutiae of scholarship, as Wilson saw it, and in the essays in this volume, perhaps ephemeral rather than substantive, he presented the sort of insightful stimulation that he saw as essential in providing intellectual leadership for a free people whom he did not underestimate.

The volume reveals, too, that Wilson's concept of American government, of America itself, and of Americans had continued to change. Perhaps most significant is his concept of the difference between English values, held by English leaders who may by accident of birth be called Americans, and values that make their holders intrinsically American, possessed of a faith in American values and democratic ideals that transcend the values of the past and provide the foundation for national greatness. Particularly important is his definition of the "great American" as the idealistic yet firm leader who attempts to transmute the ideals of the American past into the American reality of the present. Those leaders who are capable of doing so, it is evident in the essays, are those who prove major exceptions to the rules laid down in *Congressional Government,* and they anticipate the emergence of strong, progressive leadership in the next century, that in which Wilson was to reach the ideological maturity to which these personal essays, "mere literature," point the way.

V George Washington

Although *George Washington* was important to Wilson's career and his reputation, it is not a biography but a long biographical essay, as Ray Stannard Baker has pointed out (Baker II, 126). Actually, it is flawed by the nature of its initial inception and publication as a series of articles, and its emphasis and scope are further flawed by Wilson's concern for philosophical speculation on the origins, nature, and effects of Washington's background and character. Unfortunately, these concerns too often take precedence over historic fact or interpretations by reputable historians of the day; combined with a stylistic approach more suited to eulogy than to factual reporting, the result is essentially praise of Washington the man, not as a member and leader of a new breed of men, but as the best that the old tradition, transplanted to Virginia, could produce.

Nevertheless, *George Washington* is not "bad biography," as some of Wilson's later critics have maintained, and it is certainly far from William Wirt's Washington. The scholarship is derivative, as much of Wilson's always was; he was not a scholar but a philosopher and a man of letters, he insisted, and *George Washington*, with the earlier *Division and Reunion* and later *History of the American People*, all combine to support that contention. Nevertheless, Wilson's *Washington*, like his other historical writings, was not directed at his academic peers but at a much broader audience, the American people as a whole, and in this purpose, to inform, to teach, to moralize, and to interpret, his work was successful. And, of course, each work found an eager reception among America's popular intellectuals and the important Princeton alumni.

In spite of its scholarly and stylistic shortcomings, *George Washington* is less dated than one might expect. It reads well, as Wilson's prose invariably does, and it makes evident both stable and changing opinions and interpretations that contributed to Wilson's political philosophy. From the beginning it is evident that Washington's background, as Wilson perceived it, epitomized the solid English foundations of American values and patterns of behavior:

George Washington was bred a gentleman and a man of honor in the free school of Virginia society, with the generation that first learned what it meant to maintain English communities in America in safety and a self-respecting independence. He was born in a season of quiet peace, when the plot of colonial history was thickening noiselessly and almost without observation. He came to his manhood upon the first stir of revolutionary events; caught in their movement, he served a rough apprenticeship in arms at the thick of the French and Indian War; the Revolution found him a leader and veteran in affairs at forty-four; every turn of fortune confirmed him in his executive habit of foresight and mastery; death spared him, stalwart and commanding, until, his rising career rounded and complete, no man doubted him the first character of his age. "Virginia gave us this imperial man," and with him a companion race of statesmen and masters in affairs. It was her natural gift, the times and her character being what they were; and Washington's life showed the whole process of breeding by which she conceived so great a generosity in manliness and spirit.[39]

This is the attitude and tone that Wilson maintains throughout the book. Wilson devotes a great deal of attention to the background of time, place, and values that had produced Washington, and he concludes the résumé of Washington's breeding and values with the first major test of Washington's courage and determination as he carried Governor Robert Dinwiddie's letter to the French commander at Fort LeBoeuf, in western Pennsylvania, and returned to Williamsburg, in "spite of sore feet and frosts and exhausting weariness."[40]

With this precedent, Wilson insists that the course of Washington's life was set. He performed with a devotion and excellence that became the expected level of his performance. At times Wilson's eulogistic tone becomes wistful envy as, at a time when he was suffering from recurring indigestion, he recounts that "the whole disheartening work of making ready for the fight, of seeking the enemy, and of choosing a field of encounter, he had borne as a stalwart young man can while his digestion holds good."[41]

Throughout the background of revolution, independence, and the beginning of national life, Wilson focuses exclusively upon Washington, emphasizing his bearing, his skill, and his character, as he remained above the conflict and intrigue that marked the course of the War for Independence, and the same emphasis continues throughout the course of Washington's Presidency. Other characters, even including Hamilton, Adams, and Jefferson, as the course of that rivalry began to develop, are relatively minor. However, Wilson sketches the nature of Washington's response to Hamilton and Jefferson with insight:

Jefferson had slowly to discover that leadership in the cabinet was to be had, not by winning a majority of the counsellors who sat in it, but by winning Washington. That masterful man asked counsel upon every question of consequence, but took none his own judgment did not approve. He had chosen Hamilton because he knew his views, Jefferson only because he knew his influence, ability, and experience in affairs. When he did test Jefferson's views, he found them less to his liking than he had expected.[42]

Throughout the course of controversy and even growing unpopularity and public disapproval, Wilson has Washington standing firm, certain of his rightness and equally certain that that rightness will prevail, that the nation will survive, uncontaminated by the forces of French evil:

Washington's spirit was of the majestic sort that keeps a great and hopeful confidence that the right view will prevail; that the "standard to which the wise and honest will repair" is also the standard to which the whole people will rally at last, if it be but held long and steadily enough on high to be seen of all. When the moment for action came he acted promptly, unhesitatingly, as if in indifference to opinion. . . .[43]

In these last pages, Wilson is not only describing Washington as he sees him, but he is also defining a concept of the Presidency, a concept new to him and certainly lacking in his political writings from *Congressional Government* to his essays in *An Old Master and Other Political Essays*. But it was a concept of the Presidency he had been moving toward in his assessments of Grover Cleveland in the office, and in many ways it foreshadows the President who would accept a resignation that he knew was wrong. Perhaps it was ultimately this concept, when combined with his Calvinistic righteousness, that permitted him to stand firm to the end against those who would compromise the right as he saw it. And finally, again perhaps in anticipation, he concludes with a definition of the nature of greatness:

The country knew him when he was dead: knew the majesty, the nobility, the unsullied greatness of the man who was gone, and knew not whether to mourn or give praise. He could not serve them any more; but they saw his light shine already upon the future as upon the past, and were glad. They knew him now as the Happy Warrior. . . .[44]

Wilson's *George Washington* is certainly not biography, as his critics insist, but it is much more important from a personal point of view than any conventional, academically acceptable biography could possibly be. In it Wilson defines the nature, the substance, and the meaning of leadership as he has come to determine that it must be. And in that definition there is no room for the qualifications brought about by politics or intrigue, compromise or concession. The book is as much a statement of Wilson's political faith as anything that he had written before or was to write again. Unfortunately it is also one of his works most frequently ignored or overlooked, even by those who profess to understand him.

In his first publication in the new year of 1897, Wilson turned again to contemporary politics with an essay, "Mr. Cleveland as President," in the *Atlantic Monthly* for March. Written at the instigation of Walter Hines Page, it emphasizes two aspects of Cleveland's career, both of which were elements defined most clearly in his assessment of "great Americans" in his "calendar" of them. Of first consideration to Wilson were Cleveland's origins, for "it is plain that Mr. Cleveland, like every other man, had drawn his character and force in large part from his origin and breeding" (*Papers* X, 103). But for Wilson this was a particularly appropriate kind of origin and breeding, not unlike Wilson's own:

It would be easy to describe him as a man of the people, and he would, I suppose, be as proud as any other man of that peculiar American title to nobility. But . . . it is the life and associations of the family that have chiefly shaped us in our youth. Mr. Cleveland had a very definite home training: wholesome, kindly, Christian. He was bred in a home where character was disciplined and the thoughts were formed, where books were read and the right rules of life obeyed . . . he never got those first lessons, conned in plain village manses, out of his blood. . . . (*Papers* X, 103)

With such a background, firmly rooted in the values of traditional morality, those best suited for the leadership of a free people, it was evident to Wilson that Cleveland had exercised that leadership in a way unused by Presidents since Lincoln: "It cost him at least one sharp fight with the Senate to carry his purpose of executive independence into effect" (*Papers* X, 107); "he demanded tariff reform" (*Papers* X, 110); "he was the most conspicuous man in the country out of office" (*Papers* X, 111). "Once more he became President . . . he took steps to force action on the silver question" (*Papers* X, 113). "It was the President's victory that the law was at last repealed" (*Papers* X, 114). "He showed his fixed purpose . . . by the veto of the so-called Seigniorage Bill" (*Papers* X, 114); "bulked very large the while . . . in the field of foreign affairs" (*Papers* X, 116); "he showed himself a strong man" (*Papers* X, 117). "He has made policies and altered parties after the fashion of an earlier age in our history, and the men who assess his fame in the future will be no partisans, but men who love candor, courage, honesty, strength, unshaken capacity, and high purpose such as his" (*Papers* X, 119).

This is not merely the recital of the record of a President's administration, but it is a definition of the concept of the Presidency by one who believes firmly in the responsible and determined role of the political leader, one who at the same time sees it exercised for the first time in his lifetime by a President, and particularly by one of his own party. It was evident to Wilson during Cleveland's two administrations, separated by the contrasting administration of a Republican President largely distinguished by a Civil War volunteer generalcy and a Presidential name. It was evident to Wilson for the first time that the Presidency was primarily an extension of the man who occupied the office and secondarily an extension of his party.

But the Presidency, indeed any elected or appointed office, was at this time beyond Wilson's reach, and he continued his intensely active professional life. During the last years of the nineteenth century he was at his most active, much in demand as a speaker, an essayist, and a writer as well as an outstanding professor. In 1893 he had started and put aside a "Short History of the United States," a project revived in the late fall of 1897 as "A History of the United States for Schools," to be published by Harper and Brothers, and, although he began the project with that limitation in mind, it began to take on much greater proportions. He continued writing through 1899, and that fall, when Harper ran into financial difficulties and sold its educational publications and contracts to the American Book Company, Wilson requested release from the contract because his book was to be "primarily literary and not a text." The American Book Company refused to release Wilson but agreed to let the contract run indefinitely, hoping perhaps that Wilson might someday write such a book.

Meanwhile, in July 1897, Wilson published an essay, "The Making of the Nation," in the *Atlantic Monthly*. Essentially a philosophic commentary on the process of building the American nation, it emphasizes the process that has continued, largely directed and moved by self-interest and convenience rather than altruism. In the process a continental rather than regional policy had evolved, and, as Wilson concludes, a new relationship between President as leader and Congress as legislator, a new national relationship of cooperation has developed.

Although this view of the path of the future projects a continued large role for committee government by Congress, Wilson sees also a new balance emerging between executive and legislative branches, a new equality, and a new post-Cleveland role for the Presidency and for the President himself as a leader as well as an executor.

During 1898 Wilson refused a contract to write a biography of Francis Parkman for the American Men of Letters series, as he had earlier turned down the offer of a contract for a life of Daniel Webster. In April a group of alumni, aware of continued offers to Wilson of chairs and administrative positions, arranged to supplement Wilson's salary, on condition that he agree to remain at Princeton for another five years, that he minimize lectures at other universities, and that he continue his literary work. The arrangement continued until he assumed the university presidency four years later, when it became unnecessary.

In the summer of 1899 he traveled in England again, this time with his brother-in-law, Stockton Axson, to recover from a spring illness. That fall he returned to plan his history of the United States by opening discussions with Harper's again for a series of historical essays to be published in *Harper's Magazine* during 1902. This series, which began in January 1901 and concluded in December 1901, was the substance of his five-volume *History of the American People*, a project he had begun to plan when he read John Richard Green's history of England years before.

Using as a basis the draft of the school history he had written earlier as well as that of the "Short History," Wilson finished the first article by late June 1900, and he planned a total of fourteen essays rather than the twelve contracted for by Harper's. The twelve as published, however, were much more ambitious and detailed than either Wilson or Henry Mills Alden, editor of *Harper's Magazine*, had anticipated. The series ultimately ended with "The Coming of Peace," the discussion of the end of the American Revoluion.

Before all the articles were in print, Wilson began to prepare for their book publication, adding sketches and details to the original series, which was represented in the printers' copy by paste-ups of revised pages from *Harper's*. Appended to them are extensive changes, additions, and emendations in Wilson's handwriting; there are also many stylistic changes and alterations of the text as well. He continued to work intensively on the manuscript throughout 1901 and the spring of 1902. He finished the next-to-the-last chapter on May 31, 1902, and he completed the last chapter, in the midst of many distractions, after his election to the presidency of Princeton on July 3.

It was perhaps the most intensive year and a half of sustained work in Wilson's life, and he enjoyed it thoroughly. As the end came in sight in January 1902, he wrote to his friend Frederick Jackson Turner of his plans:

I was forty-five three weeks ago, and between forty-five and fifty-five, I take it, is when a man ought to do the work into which he expects to put most of himself. I love history, and think there are few things so directly rewarding and worthwhile for their own sakes as to scan the history of one's own country with all the absorbing desire to get its cream and spirit out. But, after all, I was born a politician, and must be at the task for which, by means of my historical writing, I have all these years been in training. If I finish at fifty-five, shall I not have fifteen richly contemplative years left, if the Lord be good to me! But, then, the Lord may prefer to be good to the world! (Baker II, 120)

The work that he had long planned as the best work of his life was a massive philosophy of politics, or "P.o.P.," as he called it, tentatively entitled *Statesmanship: A Study in Political Action and Leadership,* a definitive study of politics, and he planned to begin it after finishing the *History of the American People,* which, with the rest of his work, was practice, preparation, and preface to the great study. In it would go everything that he had learned and all the writing skill at his command.

To a great extent this ambition had crystallized in his thinking after his return from Europe in 1899, when he wrote a remarkable personal essay published in *Century Magazine* for June 1901 called "When a Man Comes to Himself." In it Wilson comes to terms, for perhaps the first time, with his unfulfilled and now apparently unattainable hopes for political leadership, and in general philosophic terms he examines and accepts "his own true place and function" in a world in which reality is determined by forces and factors other than dreams or desires:

. . . Every man hath both an absolute and a relative capacity: an absolute in that he hath been endowed with such a nature and such parts and faculties; and a relative in that he is part of the universal community of men, and so stands in such a relation to the whole. When we say that a man has come to himself, it is not of his absolute capacity that we are thinking, but of his relative. He has begun to realize that he is part of a whole, and to know *what* part, suitable for what service and achievement.[45]

There is no suggestion in the essay that to come to oneself meant to Wilson a loss of faith in one's self or a lessening of ambition or energy; rather it is evident that Wilson meant precisely what he had come to know and accept as the truth about himself: his role was to record and interpret, to create a literature and perhaps a philosophy of politics and history. This, he saw, was not a lesser function than that of a political activist, but a different, perhaps ultimately a more lasting, more important function. As he worked furiously on the manuscript of his history of the American people and began to plan his "P.o.P.," he had come to himself, not only for the first time, but for the last.

Further evidence of Wilson's having come to himself in an

understanding and acceptance of his role as historian is made clear in "The Significance of American History," his introduction to *Harper's Encyclopaedia of United States History*, written in the fall of 1901. In it he looks at the American past as he had so often done, and he examines the course of development of American nationhood, again as he had done in the past. But then he looks at history in a new light, as prefatory not only to the present but to the future. Here, he suggests, is the true significance of the study of history and of the role of the historian:

> The twentieth century will show another face. The stage of America grows crowded like the stage of Europe. The life of the new world grows as complex as the life of the old. A nation hitherto wholly devoted to domestic development now finds its first task roughly finished and turns about to look curiously into the tasks of the great world at large, seeking its special part and place of power. A new age has come which no man may forecast. But the past is the key to it; and the past of America lies at the centre of modern history. (*Papers*, XII, 184)

Just as Wilson had come to himself in the opening months and years of the twentieth century, he felt that the nation had done so too, and he saw his role as observer, interpreter, teacher of the nation—of those who led it, and those who were to lead it in the future. The twelve years of his professorship at Princeton had not only seen his nation and himself come to a new maturity and responsibility, but those twelve years had been years of a prodigious output of lectures, essays, books, and letters. It is possible to identify at least 100 individual speeches, talks, and lectures that he had given to audiences as disparate as church groups and the American Historical Association. In his writings and letters it is possible to identify literally hundreds of authors and books that had touched his life during those years. He had written seven books of his own and an impressive group of essays. During those years he had become a noted and incisive reviewer of the major books of his time and interests. He had become perhaps America's best known professional academic, with a following well beyond the Princeton campus or the alumni clubs. He had plans that would carry him nearly to his retirement years, when he might then relax, for the first time, after having worked so hard for so long.

As he began his final work on the last chapter of *A History of the American People* he had no idea that President Francis L. Patton was about to resign after increasing problems with his trustees and staff, and that the trustees were about to meet to select him as the first layman to become president of Princeton, thereby effectively ending the life of letters he had so recently accepted.

CHAPTER 6

The President of Princeton

WITH his election to the presidency of Princeton on July 3, 1902, and his inauguration on October 25, Woodrow Wilson began a life of action that was to continue almost without interruption for the next eighteen years, at the end of which he would retire, severely incapacitated physically, at sixty-four, with less than four years left to live. During those years, in spite of occasional wistfulness, he was no longer the man of letters which he had finally accepted as his role in human affairs. During the eighteen years of his active and public life he never wrote another book, although on several occasions he was tempted to do so, and several books were made up of his speeches and other writing.

However, in another sense he did remain the man of letters, because throughout his long, active life he refused to use a ghost writer or speech writer. Proud of his literary style, his oratorical gifts, and his ability to communicate clearly and effectively with whatever group he was facing, he prepared and wrote his own speeches, messages, letters, and papers. When one reads or studies Wilson's papers, he can be sure that he is working with Wilson's own words and thoughts. Unfortunately or not, the same thing cannot be said of many of his contemporaries or most of his successors in American public life of the twentieth century.

I A History of the American People

During the first few weeks after his election, Wilson continued work on his *History of the American People*. It was published in book form in five volumes in October 1902, in a subscription edition, a trade edition, and a limited Princeton alumni edition of 350 copies bound in orange and black. It was reprinted in 1910 in a popular edition and in a ten-volume edition, including various supplementary documents and source materials. It was widely reprinted abroad.

The reactions of professional historians at the time and since were perhaps predictable: Wilson's scholarship was neither original nor impressive, but it was, as Wilson and his publishers intended, a popular history, as well as, in general, a reliable history. The five volumes are, like his *George Washington*, more primarily historical essays of varying lengths than the sort of objective history that he had demonstrated he was capable of writing in *Division and Reunion*. It was, as John Spencer Bassett once remarked to Ray Stannard Baker, "not history, but what Woodrow Wilson thought about history" (Baker II, 126). Nevertheless, in spite of the shortcomings of the work as history, it is in the grand tradition of historical writing begun by Edward Gibbon in the eighteenth century and practiced most recently by Winston Churchill in the twentieth. Wilson's *History of the American People*, like Churchill's later *History of the English Speaking Peoples*, is an impressive piece of work.

Wilson's *History of the American People* would undoubtedly receive a harsh initial reaction from today's socially conscious younger historians, especially those neorevisionists who insist upon a multiethnic approach to American history. Wilson's history begins with a brief survey of the voyages of discovery, which he significantly entitles "Before the English Came," and then devotes the rest of Volume I to a long essay beginning with the first attempts at English exploration and settlement and ending with the English revolution of 1688. This long section, the major portion of the volume, is "The Swarming of the English."

The premise so clearly implied in this first volume is maintained throughout the rest of the history. As Wilson had insisted numerous times in the past, he based his history upon the belief that American society and institutions were, during their formative years, essentially extensions of English values, traditions, and institutions, and, although they were inevitably altered later in American history, they remained essentially English until after the American Revolution, and many of its leaders were essentially "great Englishmen," as he had pointed out before. But others, like John Adams, were something different—great American realists, and still others were like Washington, uniquely American, with changed values and habits.

Volume II is essentially the story of the transition in which the colonies, in the process of winning independence and constructing a nation, begin to alter those English traditions and values into something new. But the change itself is essentially a change that had its origins in its British influences, and the people who bring it about are Anglo-Saxons, the founders of America's English-speaking, Anglo-Saxon, Protestant tradition, that which Wilson, like so many others, had long held in trust.

Wilson's treatment of this transitional period is less chauvinistic and provincial than this résumé indicates, largely because much of the main thrust of the volume is the denial of American history as it had been written by New Englanders during much of the nineteenth century. As the new nation began its growth socially, politically, and institutionally, Wilson insisted, it was a process of a growth and expansion of all the colonies as well as a transformation of values; never was it the expansion of New England values that the young men of Harvard and Yale had described for so long.

In Volume III, "The Founding of the Nation," Wilson begins the description of a process first defined by his friend Frederick Jackson Turner at the meeting of the American Historical Society in Chicago in 1893. "The Significance of the Frontier in American History," in which Turner first advanced his "Turner Thesis," provided for Wilson the third important principle by which the course of American history and the development of American institutions might be understood. Intrinsic, then, to Wilson's definition of American history are its origins in English tradition, its continental expansion, and its great West, which made the superstructure of American greatness both possible and inevitable.

In Volumes IV and V Wilson reviewed essentially the same events of the more immediate past in the same way that he had in *Division and Reunion*. Most evident, however, in Volume IV are some changes in interpretation: a greater sympathy with Andrew Jackson, a greater admiration for Grant as a general, a greater emphasis upon Lincoln as a strong, determined President. In Volume V, devoted to the years of Reconstruction or, in Wilson's term, "rehabilitation," the emergence of nationalization, and the growth of imperialism in the Caribbean and Pacific, Wilson sees changes, sees challenge, sees hope. Perhaps of most importance in the last pages of the *History*, those which move almost imperceptibly from past to present to future, are two implications. The first of these sees paradox: as the country becomes, eagerly or not, a world power, the election of 1900 turns on essentially domestic issues, and the second is the suggestion that this will be the course of the future: greater national cohesiveness, greater concern for social progress, greater economic development. But, Wilson asserts, in so doing, America will "change the face of the world."[1]

Of more significance from Wilson's own political observations was a fact that had a great deal of significance for the future of the nation and, a decade later, for Wilson himself as he became President-elect of the United States:

It was interesting to note with how changed an aspect the government stood upon the threshold of a new century. The President seemed again to be always in the foreground, as if the first days of the government were to be repeated,—that first quarter of a century in which it was making good its right to exist and to act as an independent power among the nations of the world. Now, full grown, it was to take a place of leadership.[2]

As a whole, *The History of the American People* was a symbolically useful work with which to end one major phase of Wilson's life and to begin another. It is certainly not a work that would have been important for a man who preferred to devote his life to obscure historical scholarship, however significant it might be, but it was an important, significant, and revealing work for one who aspired to prominence and to leadership, whether on the small scale of Princeton or the much greater scale of the nation and the world. Its popular reception and reputation made Wilson's name familiar to that broad, influential, and affluent segment of the country who were not concerned with scholarship but with information, insight, and stimulation. Not only were these people those who made such a success of Wilson's history, but they were also those who were beginning to think, like Wilson himself, of the direction that American life and politics were to take in the new century.

Perhaps indicative of these very forces operating in the anonymous but powerful American middle class was a letter, suggestive, perhaps, of the beginning of the movement that took Wilson to the White House, that appeared in the *Indianapolis News* on May 5, 1902, before the *History* had been completed, although it was then running in *Harper's Magazine,* and before Wilson's election to the presidency of Princeton. Wilson had spoken twice in Indianapolis on April 26, to public schoolteachers on "The Teaching of Patriotism in the Schools," and to the Contemporary Club on "What It Means to be an American," and apparently the writer of the letter had heard him speak then.

The letter, signed "Old-Fashioned Democrat," searches for a candidate for the Democratic nomination for the Presidency among Bryan ("out of the question"), David Bennett Hill ("does not arouse enthusiasm"), and others, concluding that all are unsuitable. The man selected should be young, unidentified with past quarrels, with character and ability, and preferably a Democrat:

> . . .The type of man that I have in mind is represented by Professor Woodrow Wilson, of Princeton University, who lectured in this city a few days ago. I do not even know whether Mr. Wilson is a Democrat. . . . Mr. Wilson is a good deal more than a mere college professor. He is a man of affairs, a scholar, a patriot, and a man whose very presence inspires enthusiastic devotion. . . . (*Papers*, XII, 357)

The author may have been Louis Howland, then on the staff of the *Indianapolis News* and later its editor, and it may have been revised or abetted by Charles Richard Williams, Princeton 1875, and then editor of the *News*. Regardless of its origin, however, it was the first serious indication that Wilson was a suitable candidate for the Presidency, nearly six years before George Harvey made that suggestion at a dinner for Wilson in New York on February 3, 1906.

Whether or not Wilson was aware of this letter at the time is unknown, as is any reaction he may have made to it. But he was hard at work on the *History*; he had no idea that in a month's time he would be elected president of Princeton, and of course any suggestion that he would make a suitable Presidential candidate must have seemed completely out of the question.

However, Wilson embarked on his new presidential career with a confidence, eagerness, and enthusiasm that might have been the result of a long, expectant wait; he expressed his feeling forcefully: "How can a man who loves this place as I love it realize of a sudden that he now has the liberty to devote every power that is in him to its service?" (Baker, II, 131).

However eager Wilson may have been for his new responsibilities, Ellen Axson Wilson was much more reluctant, perhaps more aware of inherent changes, than her husband:

> Of course it involves heavy sacrifices to people of our temperament. His literary work must suffer greatly,—just how much remains to [be] seen, and we must leave our dear home and the sweet, almost ideal life when he was [a] simple "man of letters" and go and live in that great, stately troublesome "Prospect" and be forever giving huge receptions, state dinners, &c. &c. . . . (*Papers*, XII, 464)

Mrs. Wilson had perceived the nature of the change, but she could not know that the change in their pattern of living was not only great but permanent, and that for the rest of her life and almost all of her husband's they would be concerned with great dinners, great houses, and great responsibilities. Her husband would yet write his most significant works, but no longer would he be considered a "man of letters."

However, if Wilson was truly reluctant to put that phase of his life behind him, there is no record of it except a brief comment to Mrs. Edith Reid on July 12:

. . . You need give yourself no concern about the History. It was finished a couple of weeks ago (no,—one week ago) and my desks are clear; and, as for my health, that is firm and excellent. No doubt I shall have to give up writing for the next three or four years, and that is a heartbreaking thing for a fellow who has not yet written the particular thing for which he has been training all his life; but when I can tell you the circumstances I am sure that you will say that it was my duty to accept. It was a singularly plain, a *blessedly* plain, case. . . . (*Papers*, XV, 3)

II *The First Presidency*

On August 1, he cleared his desk of proofs for the history and visited his friends the Tedcastles in Clifton, Massachusetts, where he rested and began to plan his role as president and to write his presidential inaugural remarks. A few weeks earlier he had written his wife that "I feel like a new prime minister getting ready to address his constituents" (*Papers*, XV, 27) and in his speech, "Princeton for the Nation's Service," delivered on October 25, he spoke to the inaugural gathering as a prime minister addressing his party members as he outlined the course of his planning for the future.

Significantly, Wilson began by looking backward at his address, "Princeton in the Nation's Service," six years earlier, and, using the concept of the relationship between the university and nation that he had emphasized earlier as a point of departure, he first reiterated that "in planning for Princeton . . . we are planning for the country . . ." (Baker-Dodd I, I, 443), planning to provide the leadership that the nation needs:

. . . American universities serve a free nation whose progress, whose power, whose prosperity, whose happiness, whose integrity depend upon individual initiative and the sound sense and equipment of the rank and file. . . . They are not mere seminaries of scholars. They never can be. Most of them, the greatest of them and the most distinguished, were first of all great colleges before they became universities; and their task is two-fold: the production of a great body of informed and thoughtful men and the production of a small body of trained scholars and investigators. . . . (Baker-Dodd I, I, 443–44)

This concept of the nature and responsibility of the University dominated the rest of Wilson's inaugural address as well as the major portion of his presidency of Princeton, particularly in the reforms and changes that he attempted to carry through in his eight years in that office. In accepting the presidency he knew that his role would be largely political, of less significance than on the national scene, but nevertheless closely related and responsible to it. Wilson had studied and interpreted the political process throughout much of his life; now he was in a position to practice it to his utmost ability.

His concept of the presidency as that of a prime minister leading his cabinet and party seemed justified. The board of trustees gave him more power than any president had known before, and a new sense of purpose and discipline began to make itself felt. Among the first effects of this new atmosphere was his decision to expel students who cheated and to dismiss faculty members he considered weak.

Although whispers of "going too fast" and "too autocratic" began to be heard, Wilson moved forward quickly with his plan to reorganize the university upon a preceptorial system "resembling Oxford, but better than Oxford." This plan would add fifty preceptors, to function like Oxford dons, as mentors and discussants to groups of students. Furthermore, he planned to add a graduate school, an electrical-engineering school, a school of jurisprudence, and a natural-history museum. Princeton was, under his leadership, to become a great university, and he moved confidently, even raising money—a process he once decried—when necessary.

The preceptorial system was put into practice, with modifications; Wilson began a massive reorganization of the college departments, aligning them in four divisions: philosophy, art and archaeology, language and literature, and mathematics and science. Because the free-elective system then in effect had led to earlier specialization than Wilson thought wise, he set up revised basic courses for the first two years and delayed specialization until the junior year. Although enrollment dropped—fifty fewer students enrolled in the fall of 1904 than a year earlier—leading to some criticism of Wilson's policies, his first four years as president were much like those of a prime minister moving firmly and confidently through a program of change. He was strongly supported by both trustees and faculty, and a new vitalization began to be felt as first-rate scholars and teachers sought and found places on the faculty.

Although Wilson apparently thrived psychologically during these first four years, family illness and misfortune began to make inroads upon the health of his wife as well as his own. Three months after his inauguration his father, Dr. Joseph Wilson, died, and shortly thereafter, both his and his wife's health began to decline. In the summer of 1903 he took his wife abroad for the first time, for a rest. In May 1906 he suffered a slight stroke which left him temporarily blind in his left eye, and he was advised that he must retire. However, another summer in Europe restored his vision, his health, and his spirits, and he formulated new plans to enhance Princeton's growing academic reputation.

To build on his success with the preceptor system and departmental reorganization, he proposed a new living-learning plan which would establish quadrangles where students drawn from all social and academic classes would live together with members of the faculty. This, too, was based upon his observation of the English university structure.

Unfortunately the quandrangle plan meant that the eating clubs, essentially highly selective fraternities for upperclassmen, would have to be abolished. Less because they were undemocratic than because they were frivolous and antiintellectual, Wilson felt that they had no place in the university. Although the trustees accepted the plan, both faculty and alumni were strongly opposed. So strongly did Wilson feel about the issue that when his best friend on the faculty, John Grier Hibben, voted against the plan, Wilson never forgave him (Freud and Bullitt make much of both the relationship and the betrayal).

The faculty vote, swollen by Wilson's fifty preceptors, favored the new plan, but the strong alumni disapproval led the trustees to withdraw their support. Although Wilson rallied some alumni support from those who had not been members of eating clubs, the board appointed a committee of Wilson's supporters to investigate the clubs. They found nothing seriously wrong with the clubs, but conversely, lauded their effect on morality. After a hard, bitter fight marked by an abrupt rejection of compromise, Wilson lost, alienating friends among both the faculty and the trustees, including Grover Cleveland. No longer a consensus prime minister but a president fighting to lead a fragmented constituency, Wilson lost a great deal of power and prestige, while his next, most bitter controversy began to take shape. He never mentioned the quadrangle plan again.

The second controversy centered upon a new graduate school for the university. The dean of the proposed school was Andrew Fleming West, a classics scholar, who had for years advocated the establishment of such a school, based upon the British system. The school had been authorized by the trustees in 1900 and West had been chosen dean. Wilson and West had long been jealous of each other, and, although West supported Wilson's early reforms, he opposed the quadrangle plan because he felt that the money should go to establish the graduate school, which had not yet gone beyond the planning stage, largely because it had not yet been funded.

Although West had earlier outlined his plans in "The Proposed Graduate College of Princeton University" in 1903 and Wilson had written a favorable introduction to the paper, a clash was inevitable. West proposed that the college be erected apart from the university, and Wilson wanted it at the center of the campus, the focal point of his intellectual community. In 1906 West was offered the presidency of the Massachusetts Institute of Technology, and he planned to accept it, making clear to Wilson and the trustees that he would remain at Princeton only if his plans were accepted.

Instead of encouraging West to leave, by silence if not by deed or word, Wilson wrote a motion, passed by the trustees, begging West to stay because he could not be spared by the university. West remained, setting up a graduate residence off campus, but Wilson convinced the trustees that the graduate college should be built in the center of the campus; then Wilson convinced the trustees that control of the school should pass to a faculty committee of Wilson supporters.

Momentarily successful in his political maneuvers, Wilson apparently had underestimated West, who thereupon solicited a $500,000 contribution from William Cooper Procter of Cincinnati, Ohio. Procter stipulated that the college be built off the campus, and when the trustees accepted the gift, Wilson accepted the challenge directly in personal terms. On January 1, 1910, he opposed the Procter gift as a threat to the autonomy of faculty, trustees, and university:

. . . if we were to accept Mr. Procter's gift on the terms he prescribes, we should be taking the educational policy of the University out of the hands of the Trustees and Faculty. . . . We know now that Mr. Procter's gift means West's policy. . . . We give up our judgment entirely in the most essential matter of all in order to get the money. . . . We now know, indeed, that Mr.

Procter's gift is made to put West in the saddle, but we cannot make that a
matter of public discussion. We can make it public, however, that we do not
feel at liberty to accept gifts for purposes of which we disapprove. . . . (Baker
II, 320–21)

Between the writing of this letter and the meeting of the trustees
on January 13, conferences, letters, and conversations indicated that
the board of trustees was largely sympathetic to Wilson. A last-
minute compromise proposed by Moses Taylor Pyne, who opposed
Wilson on the board, was rejected in spite of the fact that the
compromise was essentially a restatement of an earlier Wilson
position. The board voted to reject the gift from Procter with his
restrictions, whereupon Procter withdrew his offer.

Wilson had won, but at enormous cost in support, harmony,
friendship, and reputation. Worn out, he sailed for Bermuda on
February 14 for a brief rest; while he was gone a storm of public
criticism broke, largely because an editorial sympathetic to Wilson
appeared in the *New York Times* on February 3, 1910. Written by H.
B. Brougham, it criticized the forces of power and wealth who
interfered with academic procedures and developed "mutually exclusive social cliques, stolid groups of wealth and fashion, devoted to
non-essentials and the smatterings of culture . . ." (Baker II, 327).

Anti-Wilson forces demanded that he repudiate the editorial and
began to talk of his forced retirement; pro-Wilson forces replied as
strongly, but Wilson regained his confidence in his actions, together
with his strength, in Bermuda. He wrote to his wife on February 21
that

we have no compromises to look back on, the record of our consciences is
clear in this whole trying business. We can be happy, therefore, no matter
what may come of it all. It would be rather jolly, after all, to start out on life
anew together, to make a new career, would it not? Experience deepens
within us. . . . (Baker II, 330–31)

Wilson's implications concerning a new career remained unclar-
ified as he returned to the university and to continued turmoil.
However, the issue was settled in May, when a wealthy alumnus,
Isaac C. Wyman, died, willing his entire estate to the university for a
graduate college, naming West as one of two executors and specifying
that the college be built according to West's ideas. Because the estate
was estimated as worth perhaps $10 million it was evident that under
the circumstances Wilson could only surrender with as much grace as

he could muster. He recommended that the gift be accepted, and it was. But of course it meant too that Wilson could not remain at Princeton.

Ironically, the bequest later turned out to be worth only $600,000, but by that time Wilson had determined to begin his new career, and on September 15, 1910, he was nominated as the Democratic candidate for governor of New Jersey. He resigned from Princeton in October.

III *Presidential Essays*

During the eight years of his presidency of Princeton, Wilson had virtually given up his conscious writing career, although he did publish several essays, including "The Ideals of America" in the *Atlantic Monthly* for December 1902; "States Rights" in the *Cambridge Modern History* in 1903; "Politics (1857–1907)" in the *Atlantic Monthly* for December 1907; "The State and Federal Government" in the *North American Review* for May 1908; "The Tariff Make-Believe" in the *North American Review* for October 1909; "What Is a College For?" in *Scribner's Magazine* for November 1909; "Hide and Seek Politics" in the *North American Review* for May 1910; and "Living Principles of Democracy" in *Harper's Weekly*, April 9, 1910. In 1908 he published another book, *Constitutional Government in the United States*, and he wrote dozens of speeches, most notably the Baccalaureate Address on June 12, 1910, his last address at Princeton.

This production certainly does not suggest that Wilson had quit writing during his years as president of Princeton, and of course he had not. The essays of the early years of his presidency, most notably "The Ideals of America," written at about the time of his accession to that office, are like his essays of the past: very consciously literary rather than scholarly or political and, like much of his work, not only informative and instructive, with a touch of the pedagogue, but also uplifting, with a touch of the moralist. Essentially "The Ideals of America" is a spin-off of his history, a re-creation of the human spirit that sought freedom and change in the American Revolution—and also in the England of that day. But it is also a most important statement of Wilson's acceptance of the old concept of Manifest Destiny and the new American imperialism and an early but significant statement of Wilson's view of an American international responsibility. Of the Revolution he writes that its leaders were revolutionists, but "the revolutionists stood for no revolution at all, but for the maintenance of accepted practices, for the inviolable understandings of precedent,—in brief, for *constitutional government*" (Baker-Dodd I, I, 422).

Wilson traces the changes—from a Hamiltonian to a Jeffersonian concept of the state and the reaffirmations, the War of 1812, and the Civil War—and he examines too the debated American responsibility to Cuba and the Philippines: "We fought but the other day to give Cuba self-government. It is a point of conscience with us that the Philippines shall have it, too, when our work is done and they are ready . . ." (Baker-Dodd I, I, 427–28). We have taken on new responsibilities, he insists, the responsibility of providing constitutional government—the very essence of free government, as Wilson saw it—to those people to whom it is still unknown. Wilson's view of American imperialism was essentially moral and visionary rather than political; it was not unlike his view of the individual leader, whether of Princeton, the nation, or the world. Firm, moral leadership must not falter, he pleads at the end, nor must we compromise. He concludes: "Let us put our leading characters at the front; let us pray that vision may come with power; let us ponder our duties like men of conscience and temper our ambitions like men who seek to serve, not to subdue, the world; let us lift our thoughts to the level of the great tasks that await us, and bring a great age in with the coming of our day of strength" (Baker-Dodd I, II, 442).

Here, at the beginning of his presidency of Princeton, long before he could possible have anticipated his political career in the governorship or the Presidency—indeed at the very time when he had concluded that his life was to be that of the writer, the teacher, the interpreter, and the moral leader rather than the political activist, Wilson gives a great deal of insight into his concept of leadership, whether it be collective or individual. To Wilson, leadership and moral responsibility are synonymous, and temptations to avoid or adulterate that responsibility are to be shunned as a Christian hermit of the early Church might fight sins of the flesh—with firmness, with sacrifice, with self-immolation, even with psychological flagellation. Above all, such a leader must not compromise, because compromise makes inevitable a responsibility not fully met. Thus, whether the issue was the structure of a university or the world, the responsibility of leadership, at whatever cost was imposed, was the same.

Implicit, too, in this essay was the beginning of an acceptance of a responsibility to lead in the active political arena if only intellectually and metaphorically, an acceptance that continued in other essays of this period: "Politics (1857–1907)," like "The Ideals of America," is a plea for responsibility at the beginning of a new age in which "our very political ideals are . . . to be decided. We are to keep or lose our place of distinction among the nations, by keeping or losing our faith in the practicability of individual liberty" (Baker-Dodd I, II, 23).

In "The Tariff Make-Believe" Wilson directly attacks the Payne-Aldrich tariff bill as an illegitimate offspring of the McKinley tariff bill and the Dingley tariff bill—illegitimate because however questionable their wisdom or validity might be, they were honest and open, whereas the Payne-Aldrich bill was not. In "Hide and Seek Politics," in an essay perhaps fortunately overlooked by his sponsors in his campaign for the New Jersey governorship, he attacked secrecy in politics, particularly that of "the unchecked power of the irresponsible politician" (Baker-Dodd I, II, 215) who had been brought to power by the secret deals of a party or a machine and a badly informed or misled electorate. Wilson demands honesty, openness, and simplicity as the means whereby governmental control can be restored to the people, and he promises a new age of political liberty when that is done.

"Living Principles of Democracy," the text of an address before members of the Democratic party of Elizabeth, New Jersey, on March 29, 1910, was both an unabashedly partisan political speech in which the party was called to unselfish, patriotic action, and a four-part statement of his own political beliefs, in which, like Lincoln at the Cooper Union, he called upon the party to make their own. He lists an abiding faith and confidence in the people and a careful regard for the lawful separation of state and federal power. The party, as he saw it, should be "at once conservative in respect of the law and radical in respect of the service we mean to render the people . . ." (Baker-Dodd I, II, 197).

Of most significance in the speech were two items all too often overlooked by those who ascribe Wilson's liberalism and his formulation of the concepts of "The New Freedom" to his meeting at Sea Girt, New Jersey, on August 18, 1912, with the young Boston lawyer and liberal, Louis Brandeis. Here Wilson makes clear the foundation of his policies as governor and the basic philosophy of "the New Freedom":

. . . It is our conviction that the interests, by which I mean the men whose energies are concentrated upon particular enterprises established under the conditions of existing law, cannot see the welfare of the country as a whole or in true proportion and perspective. . . . A third fundamental principle upon which I believe Democratic party action should rest is that the individual, not the corporation, the single living person, not the artificial group of persons existing merely by permission of the law, is the only rightful possessor alike of rights and of privileges. The corporation is a convenience, not a natural member of society. Society must be organized so that the individual will not be crushed, will not be unnecessarily hampered. Every legal instrumentality created for his convenience, like the corporation, must be created only for his convenience and never for his government or suppression. . . . (Baker-Dodd I, II, 196)

Again, Wilson sees the course of the future as the task of liberating the people from those economic combinations or political organizations that prevent them from exercising their rightful control over their government and their own affairs and, he concludes, the role of the Democratic party is to ensure that this new liberation becomes reality. To a great extent Wilson's concept is an acceptance of the direction that William Jennings Bryan had demanded that the party take.

Particularly evident in this series of essays is that fact that Wilson was increasingly concerned with his writing as a practical motivating force and decreasingly concerned with literary style. The result is a greater force and a greater sense of movement in his prose than in that of the past. Even in his ostensibly nonpolitical, nonpartisan addresses this new force and ease is evident. Thus, in "Robert E. Lee: An Interpretation," an address at the University of North Carolina on Lee's one hundredth birthday, January 19, 1901, Wilson spoke in these new tones as a prospective politician rather than a teacher, a man of letters, or a partisan:

The moral force of a country like America lies in the fact that every man has it within his choice to express the nation in himself. I am interested in historical examples as a mere historian. I was guilty myself of the indiscretion of writing a history, but if you will not let it go any further, that I wrote it, not to instruct anybody else, but to instruct myself. I wrote the history of the United States in order to learn it. That may be an expensive process for other persons who bought the book, but I lived in the United States and my interest in learning their history was, not to remember what happened, but to find which way we were going. . . . (Baker-Dodd I, II, 73)

Just a few weeks later, in Chicago, at the observance of Abraham Lincoln's one hundredth anniversary, Wilson looked first at the past and then the future:

The tasks of the future call for men like Lincoln more audibly, more imperatively, than did the tasks of the time when civil war was brewing and the very existence of the Nation was in the scale of destiny. For the things that perplex us at this moment are the things which mark, I will not say a warfare, but a division among classes; and when a nation begins to be divided into rival and contestant interests by the score, the time is much more dangerous than when it is divided into only two perfectly distinguishable interests, which you can discriminate and deal with. . . . The most dangerous thing you can have in an age like this is a man who is intense and hot. We have heat enough; what we want is light. Anybody can stir up emotions, but who is master of men enough to take the saddle and guide those awakened emotions? (Baker-Dodd I, II, 99–100)

To such an apparently rhetorical question there was, perhaps, to Wilson a logical answer which would point out the direction that his new career, so briefly and ambiguously referred to during his last months as president of Princeton, might take. And he made that suggestion in terms that were simple and direct in a situation that called not for "mere literature" but for an obviousness unobscured by eloquence or indirection.

IV   Constitutional Government in the United States

In strong contrast to the direction that his essays and addresses were taking both in style and in substance are the nature and content of *Constitutional Government in the United States,* which, appearing in 1908, was the only book published by Wilson during his presidency of Princeton. Essentially the book is the substance of a series of lectures given by Wilson at Columbia University during 1907–1908. Largely the product of his month of rest in Bermuda during January 1907, as the graduate-school controversy was taking shape, the work is much more closely related to Wilson's two studies of government, *Congressional Government* and *The State,* both of which were the product of Wilson's earlier, conservative and pedagogic years, than they are to the new activism and the practical political awareness that were beginning to become obvious in his essays and addresses.

However, of significance in the volume is the enlarged role and increased attention that Wilson gives to the office of the Presidency, both as it was defined in the Constitution and as it had evolved as the Constitution became a workable political reality. Of perhaps greater significance are his observation, of the means by which the President is selected and his analysis of a proper Presidential background as well as his conception of Presidential duties and responsibilities:

In our earlier practice cabinet officers were regarded as in the natural line of succession to the presidency; Mr. Jefferson had been in General Washington's cabinet, Mr. Madison in Mr. Jefferson's, Mr. Monroe in Mr. Madison's; and generally it was the Secretary of State who was taken. But those were days when English precedent was strong upon us, when cabinets were expected to be made up of the political leaders of the party in power; and from their ranks subsequent candidates for the presidency were most likely to be selected. The practice, as we look back to it, seems eminently sensible, and we wonder why it should have been so soon departed from and apparently forgotten. We wonder, too, why eminent senators have not sometimes been chosen; why members of the House have so seldom commanded the attention of nominating conventions; why public life has never offered itself in any definite way as a preparation for the presidential office.

If the matter be looked at a little more closely, it will be seen that the office of President, as we have used and developed it, really does not demand actual experience in affairs so much as particular qualities of mind and character which we are at least as likely to find outside the ranks of our public men as within them. What is it that a nominating convention wants in the man it is to present to the country for its suffrages? A man who will be and who will seem to the country in some sort an embodiment of the character and purpose it wishes its government to have,—a man who understands his own day and the needs of the country, and who has the personality and the initiative to enforce his views both upon the people and upon Congress. . . .[3]

Not only has Wilson's interpretation of the Presidency changed a great deal from that of *Congressional Government,* but gone also is his belief that the President should function as a prime minister, as the leader of his party, the spokesman for its policies, and the face which government presents to the governed. Rather, it is evident that Wilson had not only learned a great deal as president of Princeton about the nature and demands of leadership, but that he had come to believe that one presidency is very much like another, perhaps that one is the best preparation for another. And finally, in the conclusion of his definition of *Constitutional Government,* Wilson reiterates the nature of the relationship between government and the governed that was to become a major point in his future campaign:

Constitutional government can be vital only when it is refreshed at every turn of affairs by a new and cordial and easily attained understanding between those who govern and those who are governed . . . A people who know their minds and can get real representatives to express them are a self-governed people, the practiced masters of constitutional government.[4]

As Wilson moved toward the end of one presidency, it is evident that he thought of another, and the essence if not the substance of future campaigns had already been defined.

CHAPTER 7

The Governor of New Jersey

W OODROW Wilson's move into the active political arena was perhaps inevitable; his longtime interests and ambitions had given him a predisposition to accept if not to seek the opportunity to run for high elective office, and that opportunity became a probability rather than a remote possibility after he became president of Princeton.

Not only had his name been mentioned for the Democratic nomination for the Presidency in the election of 1904 as early as 1902, certainly then a remote possibility, but as he continued to speak publicly, he increased the numbers of those who, for one reason or another, began to think of him as a possible candidate for the Senate, the governorship, and the Presidency. The man who, more than any other, was responsible for this continued attention to a man presumably not in American public life was Colonel George Harvey, editor of *Harper's Weekly* and the *North American Review*, and an Eastern Gold Democrat.

Equally important in Wilson's emergence on the stage of elective politics was the nature of the first decade of the twentieth century. During those years Democratic populism, expounded by William Jennings Bryan, and Republican progressivism, defined by Theodore Roosevelt, had dominated the respective parties in spite of stirring opposition in each. Perhaps more importantly, progressivism had captured the popular imagination. Although Bryan did not achieve the Presidency and Roosevelt had become an accidental President, the forces of reform, based on the American traditions of natural rights, democratic control of government, and romantic social reform, had begun to assert themselves in response to the close alliance that had emerged in the 1870s and 1880s between conservative
100

government and the great concentrations of power and wealth that had come to characterize American business and industry in the post–Civil War years.

During these decades and, in particular, the Princeton years, Wilson presented a conservative public image. Not only did he refuse to support Bryan in 1896, but he supported Eastern Gold Democratic candidates. As Roosevelt emerged as a progressive, Wilson expressed his disapproval of Roosevelt's role as a governmental policeman, wielding a stick as large and as coercive on America's domestic scene as in international affairs. He believed firmly that coercion and punishment were wrong; that moral suasion and leadership, combined with personal rather than corporate punishment of individual wrongdoers, would be sufficient to regenerate America.

Apparently Colonel Harvey had decided, as early as 1902, that Wilson, a gold Democrat, a moralist, and a conservative would make a suitable Democratic candidate, and on February 3, 1906, at a dinner given in honor of Wilson by the Lotos Club in New York, Harvey made his support public. Rising, Colonel Harvey declared that it would give him the greatest pleasure if he could anticipate "even the remotest possibility of voting for Wilson to become President of the United States." The following year, 1907, Harvey proposed Wilson for Senator from New Jersey, but the legislature remained in Republican hands, and, in those pre–seventeenth amendment days, they chose one of their own.

The degree to which Wilson took these proposals seriously is impossible to tell, but Harvey's influence led other editors, publishers, and politicians to begin to regard Wilson as a possible candidate who would give moral support to reform while withholding political or legal force. In 1910, as Wilson gained a popular reputation as a democratic reformer in academia at the expense of his security of tenure as president of Princeton, it appeared to Harvey that he might launch Wilson's political career as Democratic candidate for the governorship of New Jersey.

New Jersey in 1910 had a well-justified reputation for corruption and machine- and boss-controlled politics. From 1869 to 1893 the state had been dominated by a corrupt Democratic machine, which was replaced by an equally corrupt Republican machine in 1893. New Jersey corporation laws were lax, and the state was nominal headquarters for a good many industrial empires. In 1910, small Progressive elements in both parties, led by George L. Record among the Republicans and Joseph P. Tumulty among the Democrats, were vocal centers of opposition but no real threat to continued machine control.

To secure Wilson's nomination, Harvey approached James Smith Jr., his friend, former United States Senator, and Democratic boss of Trenton and Essex County. Easily convinced that such a prominent candidate could be elected, and as a neophyte in politics could easily be controlled, Smith consented to persuade other Democratic bosses to support Wilson. Perhaps, too, Harvey suggested a possible Democratic capture of the state legislature and a return to Washington for Smith. Perhaps Harvey even suggested a kingmaker role for Smith in the national convention of 1912. Smith worked hard, but without assurances from his candidate, other Democratic bosses, notably Robert Davis of Jersey City, were reluctant to trust a man who presented such a righteous image.

While Harvey maneuvered, Wilson had apparently been attracted to his possible candidacy at first but then lost his enthusiasm. Finally, however, on the evening of June 26, 1910, Smith and Wilson met at Harvey's home; there was much talk of 1912, and Wilson consented to run, later announcing publicly that to accept a nomination would be a duty and an honor. He also agreed privately that he was not a prohibitionist and not a practical politician. As such, he agreed that matters of party policy would remain in experienced hands, that he would listen to their counsel, and that he would expect their support in matters of policies, measures, and men.

Wilson was certainly not the naive neophyte that some of the bosses, including Smith, apparently assumed. Not only had he proved his political talents and interests as president of Princeton, but it is evident that his interests were already moving beyond the state house in Trenton. Although he publicly quoted Mr. Dooley to the effect that "If anny Dimmicrat has a stiddy job he'd better shtick to it" (Baker III, 62), he had already on June 17 described the plans for the course of the future to a friend, confidant, and supporter on the Princeton board of trustees: "It is immediately, as you know, the question of my nomination for the governorship of New Jersey; but that is the mere preliminary of a plan to nominate me in 1912 for the presidency . . ." (Baker III, 56). At the same time, not only did he solicit advice from Smith and his friends, but at the heart of the solicitation is an implied request for support.

In spite of the controversy surrounding his announced candidacy—progressives and labor unions opposed, while the sensational *New York Journal* for July 8, 1910, announced, "Wall St. to Put

Up W. Wilson For President," Wilson was nominated overwhelmingly for the governorship in the party convention in Trenton on September 15.

I *The First Political Speech*

Wilson walked onto the stage of the Taylor Opera House in Trenton the candidate of the party bosses of the Democratic party of New Jersey; he left it a few minutes later the candidate of the party, including the handful of Progressives. He began, confidently and clearly, in conventional terms: "You have conferred upon me a very great honour. I accept the nomination you have tendered me with the deepest gratification that you should have thought me worthy to lead the Democrats of New Jersey in this stirring time of opportunity" (Baker III, 78).

From this point, however, the speech took a turn not anticipated by any of the factions present, and accounts of immediate reaction ranged from exultation to fury: "As you know, I did not seek this nomination. It has come to me absolutely unsolicited, with the consequence that I shall enter upon the duties of the office of Governor, if elected, with absolutely no pledges of any kind to prevent me from serving the people of the State with singleness of purpose. Not only have no pledges of any kind been given, but none have been proposed or desired" (Baker III, 79).

This was not the acceptance speech of a prime minister, the spokesman of a unified party and the leader of a disciplined unit; this was the declaration of a determined leader, dedicated to the service of the ultimate authority of a democratic society rather than to the purpose of those who sought to manipulate the public trust for their own ends. He continued in tones reminiscent of the same call to service and evocation of vision that he had used at Princeton on October 21, 1896, and again on October 25, 1902, and June 12, 1910. At the same time his remarks anticipated the great Presidential speeches of March 4, 1913, March 5, 1917, and at the joint session of Congress on April 2, 1917. He went on:

The future is not for parties playing politics, but for measures conceived in the largest spirit, pushed by parties whose leaders are statesmen not demogogues, who love, not their offices but their duty and their opportunity for service. We are witnessing a renaissance of public spirit, a reawakening of sober public opinion, a revival of the power of the people, the beginning of an age of a thoughtful reconstruction that makes our thought hark back to the great age in which democracy was set up in America. With the new age we shall show a new spirit. We shall serve justice and candour and all things that make for right. Is not our own ancient party the party disciplined and made ready for this great task? Shall we not forget ourselves in making it the instrument of righteousness for the State and the Nation? (Baker III, 79)

In his appeal not to the party which had nominated him but the party which he saw as his own righteous democratic instrument, Wilson found two of his most loyal future supporters, Joseph P. Tumulty, who was to serve as his confidential private secretary during the Presidency, and John W. Wescott, who had opposed Wilson so strongly that he had not stayed for his speech, but later studied it so carefully at his brother's instigation that he supported him wholeheartedly, nominating him for the Presidency in 1912 and again in 1916.

As brief as it was, the speech was Wilson's most forceful and eloquent in the governorship race. After the convention he emerged a popular political leader, a confident candidate, and the front runner in the election. Only in the background could Mrs. Wilson's murmur be heard: "I can see that our beautiful private life is gone." Never again in her lifetime was Woodrow Wilson to be a private citizen, and never again was he free of public issues, of grand visions, and of a concept of leadership uniquely his.

However, the substance and the force of the speech need not have been surprising either to the machine politicians, to whom it threatened betrayal, or to the Progressives, who found it hopeful. Not only had Wilson made clear his concepts of duty and responsibility in leadership on countless occasions as an essayist, a lecturer, and an academic politician, but the thrust of his impetus toward reform had also been made known publicly, particularly on two occasions: in a speech in St. Louis in 1907 when he urged his audience to reform city politics, and more significantly, when he addressed the annual convention of the American Bankers' Association in Denver on September 30, 1908. In that speech, while sympathetic, he was blunt:

I am sure that many bankers must have become acutely and sensitively aware that the most isolated and the most criticized interest of all is banking. The banks are, in the general view and estimation, the special and exclusive instrumentalities of capital used on a large scale. They stand remote from the laborer and the body of the people, and put whatever comes into their coffers at the disposal of the captains of industry, the great masters of finance, the corporations which are in the way to crush all competitors. . . . (Baker-Dodd I, II, 58)

Whether true or not—and Wilson acknowledged that in large part it was false—that was the popular view of banking; and the resolution of it was their own responsibility through social awareness and responsible action: "We cannot shut ourselves in as experts to our own business. We must open our thoughts to the country at large and serve the general intelligence as well as the general welfare" (Baker-Dodd I, II, 63). Like the university, in other words, Wilson saw the financial establishment as necessarily responsible for the public good and the public service; in the former case, Wilson's implication was clear: the university could serve or become inconsequential; in this case, it was equally clear: the banking community could serve the people voluntarily, or the choice would be taken out of their hands by an aroused electorate, however misinformed it might be.

Wilson's campaign for the governorship, his success, and his two-year administration in Trenton belong properly to political and social history rather than to literary history. Nevertheless, his public campaign speeches were noted for force, eloquence, and a quick wit. On one occasion early in the campaign, for example, Wilson quickly took advantage of a situation to give a measure of humor and life to a campaign that might have remained humorless and dull. In a speech at Jersey City, he was speaking with great seriousness, when a man in the audience called out, "Go it, Woody. You are all right. But you ain't no beaut."[1]

Quickly Wilson responded with the limerick that was to become famous:

> For beauty I am not a star;
> There are others handsomer, far;
>   But my face, I don't mind it,
>   For I am behind it;
> 'Tis the people in front that I jar.[2]

But the campaign and the governorship were far more than exercises in wit; they were learning experiences in two areas: in the art of campaign and political speaking, and in the art of developing and articulating political principles. The first lesson came early, in a speech at Jersey City on September 28. At first, apparently embarrassed, he stumbled, hesitated, told an irrelevant story. Then, with an air of earnestness, he began: "I never before appeared before an audience and asked for anything, and now I find myself in the novel position of asking you to vote for me for governor of New Jersey . . ." (Baker III, 87). His conclusion was equally direct and personal: "And so, gentlemen, I have made my first political plea. I feel that I am before a great jury. I don't want the judge to butt in. I am content to leave the decision in your hands" (Baker III, 87).

Response was good, but Wilson had not yet learned what should go between the beginning and the end. His speeches were "mere academic lectures on government," according to the reformers, who demanded a stand on direct primaries, on a corrupt practice act and employers' liability acts, as well as an attack on bossism. Gradually Wilson drew away from the bosses, especially Smith, on the issue of local option, which they saw as politically expedient, and Wilson as an infringement on personal liberty. Finally, however, two weeks before the election, stung by the accusation by former governor John Griggs that he was "a man of the library" without political experience, Wilson challenged any politician to public debate. George L. Record, then running for Congress as a Progressive Republican, accepted.

After a further exchange, Record sent Wilson a series of nineteen questions focusing on the role of political bosses and money interests in the campaign. Although advised by his friends not to reply and thus commit himself publicly and perhaps endanger party support from the regulars and their friends, Wilson was determined to answer clearly and completely, and he did so. On bossism especially, questions and answers were pointed:

Q. Do you admit that the boss system exists as I have described it? If so, how do you propose to abolish it?

A. Of course I admit it. Its existence is notorious. I have made it my business for many years to observe and understand that system, and I hate it as thoroughly as I understand it. You are quite right in saying that the system is bi-partisan; that it constitutes "the most dangerous condition in the public life of our state and nation to-day," and that it has, for the time being, "destroyed representative government, and in its place set up a government of privilege." I would propose to abolish it by the above reforms, by the election of men to office who will refuse to submit to it and bend all their energies to break it up, and by pitiless publicity. (Baker III, 98)

Wilson was equally forthright in his responses to questions dealing with specific bosses—Democrats James Smith Jr., James R. Nugent, and Bob Davis as well as Republicans David Baird, Franklin Murphy, John Kean, and E. C. Stokes—and with questions concerning the problems of public utilities, trusts, and corporations. He advocated state control of utilities, workmen's compensation, and the direct election of United States Senators. He supported a corrupt-practices act, although he refused to demand that other candidates sign pledges of support for reform.

With these responses, regarded somewhat cynically by Smith and other bosses, Wilson learned for the first time that the campaign demanded specific platforms and programs rather than education in political theory, and he found that he was prepared to provide those specifics. And in so doing he made it clear that he was aligned firmly with the Progressives of his party, committed to a social reform he had often addressed in moral generalities, but never before in such specific detail. In his last speech of the campaign, on November 5, he declared war on special interest, and at the same time he gave insight into the attitude that led him to his last massive speaking campaign nine years later:

We have begun a fight that, it may be, will take many a generation to complete, the fight against special privilege, but you know that men are not put into this world to go the path of ease; they are put into this world to go the path of pain and struggle. No man would wish to sit idly by and lose the opportunity to take part in such a struggle. All through the centuries there has been this slow, painful struggle forward, forward, up, up, a little at a time, along the entire incline, the interminable way. . . .

What difference does it make if we ourselves do not reach the uplands? We have given our lives to the enterprise, and that is richer and the moral is greater. (Baker III, 105)

Wilson returned to Princeton that evening unaware that he would not only win but by the biggest majority given any candidate for governor with one exception: 49,056 votes. In a state solidly Republican for the past seventeen years, he carried a Democratic legislature with him, and to cheering Princeton students he said, "It is my ambition to be the governor of all the people, and render to them the best service I am capable of rendering" (Baker III, 106).

II *Inaugural Address as Governor*

In his inaugural address as governor of New Jersey, not only was Wilson at his most eloquent but he was clearly the reformer, perhaps newly enlisted, but dedicated. He begins with a description of change, anticipating that which would later provide the basis for the New Freedom:

> The opportunity of our day in the field of politics no man can mistake who can read any, even the most superficial, signs of the times. We have never seen a day when duty was more plain, the task to be performed more obvious, the way in which to accomplish it more easy to determine. The air has in recent months cleared amazingly about us. . . . The whole world has changed within the lifetime of men not yet in their thirties; the world of business, and therefore the world of society and the world of business. . . . (Baker-Dodd I, II, 270–71)

Perhaps most telling was Wilson's description of the trusts and corporations, not as organizations beyond understanding and hence beyond control, but as the creations of men and hence comprehensible and controllable by other men:

> Corporations are no longer hobgoblins which have sprung at us out of some mysterious ambush, nor yet unholy inventions of rascally rich men, nor yet the puzzling devices by which ingenious lawyers build up huge rights out of a multitude of small wrongs; but merely organizations which have proved very useful but which have for the time being slipped out of . . . control. . . . We have now to set ourselves to control them, soberly but effectively, and to bring them thoroughly within the regulation of the law.
>
> There is a great opportunity here; for wise regulation, wise adjustment, will mean the removal of half the difficulties that now beset us in our search for justice and equality and fair chances of fortune for the individuals who make up our modern society. . . . (Baker-Dodd, I, II, 271–72)

Wilson uses some detail, both in descriptions of areas of needed legislation and in possible models of legislation; unlike his earlier political addresses, it is evident that he has learned to be direct and specific rather than general and visionary, and in some cases his charges to the legislature are quite pointed. But his conclusion is that of Wilson the dedicated leader:

> We are servants of the people, of the whole people. Their interest should be our constant study. We should pursue it without fear or favor. Our reward will be greater than that to be obtained in any other service: the satisfaction of furthering large ends, large purposes, of being an intimate part of that slow but constant and ever hopeful force of liberty and of enlightenment that is lifting mankind from age to age to new levels of progress and achievement,

and of having been something greater than successful men. For we shall have been instruments of humanity. . . . (Baker-Dodd I, II, 281)

Wilson's program and vision were prefatory to a year that was perhaps busier than any he had known before but, as Ray Stannard Baker comments, "Reading the immense correspondence of those years, one doubts whether Wilson was ever happy. Stern joy, the glory of victory, the high satisfaction of duty well done, he felt often: happiness rarely, or never" (Baker III, 154). To a friend during that first hectic year of the governorship, he wrote:

Truly, I know what "public life" is now! I have no private life at all. It is entertaining to see the whole surge about you . . . but when a fellow is like me—when, i.e., he *loves* his own privacy, loves the liberty to think of his friends . . . and to dream his own dreams . . . rebellion comes into his heart and he flings about like a wild bird in a cage. . . . Where and when does one's own heart get a chance to breathe. . .? (Baker III, 155–56)

Nevertheless, during that first year as governor of New Jersey, it is evident that Wilson had found both a sense of duty and an exhilaration, the combination of which was perhaps the closest he could come to true happiness, and he seemed to thrive on the challenge and the sense of accomplishment that he felt.

Wilson's first year as governor provided the substance out of which reform ambitions and programs are made: he refused to support Smith for Senator and instead supported James E. Mortine, a political amateur; he forced through the Geran Act, a primary-election bill; he created a public-utilities commission empowered to set rates and regulate practices; he set up an accident-insurance system under workmen's compensation; he supported a corrupt-practices act. Then he turned to campaigning for local reform.

However, in the election of 1911, a Republican victory produced a hostile legislature. Forced to veto fifty-seven bills, Wilson found more partisan opposition at the same time that he began to speak outside the state, obviously making known his availability and suitability for the nomination for the Presidency in 1912. Criticized, with some justification, for neglecting state business, he turned increasingly to a group of young, largely amateur supporters, among them Joseph P. Tumulty, now his secretary and devoted supporter. In the background, Colonel Harvey began to gather his forces: party bosses in New York, Indiana, and Illinois; anti-Bryan forces, particularly among businessmen; and a growing number of Democratic

Progressives. With a growing split in the Republic party, Harvey saw
a Democratic victory taking shape, and he was determined that it
would be Wilson's.

CHAPTER 8

The President and the New Freedom

AS the Presidential election of 1912 approached, it was evident that it would be at once perhaps the most predictable and at the same time the most complex election since that of 1860. If it was to be a Democratic year, as 1860 had been a Republican year, the major question was the identity of that Democrat. And if the Republican party was to split between two elements as the Democratic party did in 1860, what effect would Roosevelt, a powerful, popular leader in 1912, have upon the fortunes and future not only of his own party but upon those of the opposition and of the nation at large?

As the party conventions neared, Wilson had alienated the conservatives in the coalition put together by Colonel Harvey. He rejected William Randolph Hearst's offer of support, and he began, largely at Mrs. Wilson's instigation, to repair some of the damage resulting from his earlier refusal to support William Jennings Bryan. Not only did he make peace with Bryan but he pointed out that he had voted for him in 1900 and 1908. Clearly on the side of the Progressives, he fell under attack by the conservative Democrats, and eventually Colonel Harvey withdrew his support.

At the convention, which began on June 25 in Baltimore, Wilson faced Champ Clark of Missouri, Speaker of the House, and a Populist who attracted conservative support; Oscar W. Underwood of Alabama, chairman of the House Ways and Means Committee, a Southerner and conservative; and Governor Judson Harman of Ohio, a conservative who stood waiting in the wings.

In the meanwhile, in Chicago the Republicans, as predicted, had split; Roosevelt, crying fraud, had bolted, taking with him nearly half of the delegates and most of the confidence and glamour of the party, leaving William Howard Taft to a nomination that had lost its value. The Democrats, with victory in sight, prepared for a convention that might, however, be fratricidal, with Bryan's considerable power as yet uncommitted. Insisting upon a Progressive keynote speaker,

111

Bryan found support only from Wilson. Although Clark had carried most of the primaries and entered the convention with a solid array of votes, Wilson became at once the candidate of Democratic progressivism and the man to watch. Shrugging off the embarrassment of antiforeign, anti-immigrant, antiunion quotations from the past, many of them taken out of context by Hearst and others, Wilson made clear his progressivism.

On the first, predictable ballot, Clark received 440½ votes, Wilson 324; Harmon 148; and Underwood 117½, and there was a scattering of others, including one for Bryan. Positions remained essentially unchanged until the tenth ballot, when New York's 90 votes moved from Harmon to Clark, giving Clark a majority but not the two-thirds necessary to win. No candidate with a majority had ever failed to win, however, and as Clark prepared his acceptance speech, Wilson wired his managers to release his delegates.

However, his managers, William G. McAdoo and William F. McCombs, refused to give up. Together with Underwood's men, they conspired to block Clark. On the fourteenth ballot, Bryan switched his vote to Wilson, and gradually other Bryan men did the same thing. After a Sunday recess, Wilson moved ahead of Clark on the thirtieth ballot; he won a majority on the forty-second. The next day, on the forty-sixth ballot, Underwood threw his delegates to Wilson. As he accepted the nomination, a declared Progressive, Wilson began to formulate plans for a winning program.

By the middle of August 1912, it was evident that the contest was between Wilson and Roosevelt, the nominee of the new Progressive, or Bull Moose, party. With the backing of Progressives and reformers as diverse as Jane Addams of Hull House and George L. Record of New Jersey, the Progressive party had met, sung "Onward, Christian Soldiers," listened to Roosevelt at his dynamic best, adopted a platform that supported a minimum wage for women, prohibition of child labor, workmen's compensation, and social insurance. Politically, they demanded a national Presidential primary, full public disclosure of political financing, a federal trade commission, and a tariff commission. Describing the platform as "a statement of social and economic principles that was a classic synthesis of the most advanced thought of the time,"[1] Roosevelt declared war not only on Taft, who by this time knew that he could only run to stop Roosevelt, but also on Wilson, whose Progressive credentials were to Roosevelt always fraudulent.

Roosevelt's platform became known as "The New Nationalism";

Wilson emerged from conferences at Sea Girt, New Jersey, with what was called "The New Freedom." Although to William Allen White and others the issue was between Tweedledee and Tweedledum, there were basic philosophical and practical differences.

Roosevelt's program was strongly influenced by Herbert Croly's *The Promise of American Life*, while Wilson's ideas had largely been systematized through the influence of Louis D. Brandeis. Croly's thesis, essentially a summary of advanced progressivism, was an attempt to draw from the competing Jeffersonian and Hamiltonian traditions in American political thought the best and most suitable aspects of each for the benefit of the people. Thus, to Croly, Hamiltonian nationalism meant interference by government in the economic realm for the benefit of the wealthy and powerful; Jeffersonian Democracy was based largely on weak central government and *laissez-faire* policies.

To Croly, and later to Roosevelt, the solution to the problems of controlling economic power was to accept the Jeffersonian ends, traditionally liberal, and the Hamiltonian means, traditionally conservative, as the Progressive program. In a speech at Osawatomie, Kansas, on August 31, 1910, Roosevelt first made known his acceptance of these ideas as he denounced the old nationalism, the tool of special interests, and proposed the new nationalism, a powerful central government that would bring corporations under government control for the benefit of all, while directing the use of private property for the well-being of all. As Roosevelt moved into his campaign, first for the Republican nomination and then for the Presidency as Progressive party candidate, he became more precise in detail. At the same time, he attacked Wilson as the representative of an archaic Jeffersonian *laissez-faire*. Wilson represented, to Roosevelt, an old-fashioned "rural Toryism."

On the other hand, Wilson's "New Freedom" was based upon a continued free-enterprise policy, long advocated by Brandeis. As the New Freedom came into focus it emphasized freeing business from the shackles of monopoly and special interest, thus creating a truly free economic system within a truly free society, for the benefit of all. Remedial legislation rather than government control was the means whereby Wilson would set business free.

Just as Roosevelt attacked Wilson for the comparatively traditional nature of his views, Wilson attacked Roosevelt as paternalistic, as advocating government by government commissioner, as denying Americans the freedom they deserved and wanted. As the campaign came to its climax Wilson became convinced that Roosevelt threatened a return to slavery, whereas he insisted that his program was an extension of democracy into the economic realm. Increasingly Wilson seemed more dedicated and sincere; many Progressives began to question Roosevelt's sincerity; and each candidate began to see the other in increasing bitter personal terms. The tariff issue, with which Wilson began his campaign, had, by the end, virtually disappeared.

The results of the election were clearly a mandate for Progressive policies: Wilson received 6,293,019 popular votes; Roosevelt, 4,119,507; Taft, 3,484,956; and Eugene Debs, the Socialist candidate, 901,873. In the electoral college, Wilson won with the traditional electoral landslide: 435 votes. Roosevelt won 88, while Taft carried only Vermont and Utah, for eight votes. The Democrats also took control of Congress, the House by 73 votes, and the Senate by six.

The mandate was clear, but its direction and dimensions were uncertain, although it was equally clear that the victory entitled Wilson to claim the leadership of political progressivism in the United States. Nevertheless, Wilson's basic political philosophy in the campaign emphasized free competition in a free market, and he was obligated to construct a political program that would enable truly free competition to dominate the American economy. In essence, Wilson's New Freedom, as defined in the course of the campaign, insisted that it was applying traditional Democratic principles to new situations.

The record of Wilson's speeches in the campaign of 1912 appeared in two forms: initially in Wilson's *The New Freedom,* which was first published serially in the *World's Work,* from January to July 1913, and then in book form, also in 1913, by Doubleday, Page and Company. Both forms comprise Wilson's campaign speeches as edited by William Bayard Hale, a former clergyman who had written Wilson's official campaign biography: *Woodrow Wilson: The Story of His Life.* However, it was not until 1956 that the full texts of Wilson's 1912 speeches were published in *A Crossroads of Freedom,* edited by John Wells Davidson from transcriptions of the shorthand notes of Charles L. Sivem in the Wilson Papers, the transcripts made by Mrs. Inez C. Fuller, and other sources. Of the two versions of the speeches, the Davidson version is by far the more complete; *The New Freedom* is the more coherent, as well as that which Wilson did approve.

A number of Wilson critics and biographers have regretted that Wilson did not write the book on politics that he might have written during or after his Presidency, and neither his campaign nor Presidential speeches can actually substitute for such a volume, not only because they are the product of immediate political demands rather than the reflective analysis of which Wilson was capable but also because in many respects the speeches are tentative tests or definitions that Wilson might or might not have included in any definitive statement. However unsatisfactory the speeches are as substitutes, nevertheless, they have their own value as measures of Wilson's attempts to articulate some of his new ideas and to make them tangible.

I   The New Freedom

In *The New Freedom* the edited collection loses some of its immediacy; the order in which the speeches were given is altered, and only about one-fourth of the total number and length of campaign speeches is included, but in his preface Wilson defines the book's purpose:

The book is not a discussion of measures or of programs. It is an attempt to express the new spirit of our politics, and to set forth, in large terms which may stick in the imagination, what it is that must be done if we are to restore our politics to their full spiritual vigor again, and our national life, whether in trade, in industry, or in what concerns us only as families and individuals, to its purity, its self-respect, and its pristine strength and freedom. The New Freedom is only the old revived, and clothed in the unconquerable strength of modern America.[2]

Like Davidson's edition of the speeches, those in *The New Freedom* are, according to Wilson's preface, largely reconstructed from stenographic reports, probably those by Charles L. Sivem. Wilson comments that "I have not tried to alter the easy-going and often colloquial phraseology in which they were uttered from the platform, in the hope that they would seem the more fresh and spontaneous because of their very lack of pruning and recasting,"[3] and it appears that the differences between the texts are essentially insignificant, being the result of variant readings of the shorthand notes rather than any significant recasting either by Hale or by Davidson. For example, in Chapter 2 of *The New Freedom,* the second paragraph reads:

That is a parable of progress. The laws of this country have not kept up with the change of economic circumstances in this country; they have not kept up with the change of political circumstances; and therefore we are not even where we were when we started. We shall have to run, not until we are out of breath, but until we have caught up with our own conditions, before we shall be where we were when we started; when we started this great experiment which has been the hope and the beacon of the world. And we should have to run twice as fast as any national program I have seen in order to get anywhere else.

I am, therefore, forced to be a progressive. . . .[4]

Conversely, the same paragraph in the context of the speech in which it was given, on September 25, 1912, in Hartford, Connecticut, reads:

Now, that is to my mind the image of progressivism. The laws of this country have not kept up with the change of economic circumstances in this country; they have not kept up with the change of political circumstances in this country; and therefore we are not where we were when we started. And we will have to run, not until we are out of breath, but until we have caught up with our own conditions, before we shall be where we were when we started; when we started this great experiment which has been the hope of the world. And we would have to run twice as fast as any rational progressive program I have seen in order to get anywhere else.

I am, therefore, a progressive because. . . .[5]

Differences between the two texts are largely those of changes of tenses and transitions because of the changed circumstances and a few other details, perhaps the result of accident on the part of the speaker, the shorthand recorder, the transcriber, or the editor. With such a number of possible sources of error, differences are certainly not useful for comments on stylistic changes, nor, indeed, for comments on Wilson's style. However, Hale unfortunately did not see, or chose not to see, those possibilities in his later criticism of Wilson's style, *The Story of a Style*.

If the texts of Wilson's speeches in either context tell us little that can be considered conclusive about Wilson's style at the time, they tell us a great deal about Wilson's thinking as he sought the Presidency in 1912, and the more logical sequence of these ideas appears in *The New Freedom*, as the speeches are arranged in an order that proceeds from the simple and abstract to the complex and detailed. Whether Hale or Wilson is responsible for this arrangement is most unimportant; the ideas are certainly not Hale's but Wilson's.

The first chapter of *The New Freedom* is an attempt to define the foundations of contemporary American society. In it, Wilson asserts that "we are in the presence of a new organization of society," one in which "the old political formulas do not fit the present problems," and most importantly, "the new order of society has not been made to fit and provide the convenience or prosperity of the average man. . . ."[6] The essence of this new society is its impersonality: "Today the everyday relationships of men are largely with great impersonal concerns, with organizations, not with other individual men. . . ."[7]

This concept, a half century before its definition in the midcentury's *The Organization Man,* is the essence of the problem inherent in the new age, as Wilson sees it, and much of his program, much of the responsibility that he insists is inherent in representative government, is to humanize it; humanization of business and industry, as Wilson saw it, could come only through a renewed recognition of human individuality. And this restoration, he was convinced, could come about only through the specific social reforms that made up *The New Freedom.* In terms reminiscent of the early nineteenth-century romantic reformers, particularly Emerson and Thoreau, he addresses himself to the origins of the social evils of the twentieth century:

So what we have to discuss is, not wrongs which individuals intentionally do,—I do not believe there are a great many of those,—but the wrongs of a system. I want to record my protest against any discussion of this matter which would seem to indicate that there are bodies of our fellow-citizens who are trying to grind us down and do us injustice. There are some men of that sort. I don't know how they sleep o' nights, but there are men of that kind. Thank God, they are not numerous. The truth is, we are all caught in a great economic system which is heartless. The modern corporation is not engaged in business as an individual. When we deal with it, we deal with an impersonal element, an immaterial piece of society. . . .[8]

Evil, then, the social evil that brought progressivism into existence, was, in terms typical of the American social reformer, institutional rather than personal, and the implications are clear: if one would save men, he must change the institutions, and, of course, make them personally responsive and responsible rather than permit them to remain impersonally dominating merely because they may be "good," as Roosevelt's "New Nationalism" continued to insist.

A particularly significant aspect of Wilson's definition of evil, however, is an aspect that was to become very important in his later battles with members of the Senate over ratification of the Peace Treaty with Germany and acceptance of an unfettered League of Nations. That aspect, certainly a remnant of Wilson's Calvinist heritage, is that at the heart of this institutional evil, there are evil men—certainly not the great majority, as Calvin would insist; Wilson was too much of a democrat to see human evil as being widespread, as Calvin insisted it was—but a handful who are so willful that they must be exposed, so that the great majority can reject them and their works. Much of Wilson's determined opposition to Dean West and others at Princeton was based upon that conviction; his vision of the war as a great crusade for mankind was another; and so was the struggle over the League with Henry Cabot Lodge. In each case compromise was impossible because evil was absolute, and, in Wilson's view, so was the good served by virtuous people everywhere. In the final analysis, Wilson believed, one could take the case to the people—at Princeton, in domestic politics, in presenting the "Fourteen Points," in fighting Vittorio Orlando and Georges Clemenceau, and ultimately, in saving the League. In each case the people would recognize good when it was explained to them, and they would support it.

Much of the rest of *The New Freedom* and of the speeches of the campaign are essentially Wilson's attempt to carry the truth to the people, so that they might act. "We stand in the presence of a revolution," he writes, "not a bloody revolution; America is not given to the spilling of blood,—but a silent revolution, whereby America will insist upon recovering in practice those ideals which she has always professed, upon securing a government devoted to the general interest and not to special interests."[9] Here, too, Wilson presents his curious combination of romanticism and Calvinism as he looks back to a time, an ideal, and a way of life that was pure and uncorrupted.

Wilson follows his declaration of revolution with an attempt to define the nature of progress as he, a determined Progressive, sees it. Here, too, the essentially nonrevolutionary, nonradical nature of progressivism is made clear as Wilson rejects change for its own sake as well as massive reconstruction of the system. All progress is change, he makes clear, but not all change is progress: "Change is not worth while for its own sake. I am not one of those who love variety for its own sake. If a thing is good today, I should like to have it stay that way tomorrow."[10]

However, significantly, Wilson sees the change inherent in society as organic change, change which can be understood and controlled for good by human minds:

> . . . Living political constitutions must be Darwinian in structure and in practice. Society is a living organism and must obey the laws of life, not of mechanics; it must develop.
>
> All that the progressives ask or desire is permission—in an era when "development," "evolution," is the scientific word—to interpret the Constitution according to the Darwinian principle; all they ask is recognition of the fact that a nation is a living thing and not a machine. . . .[11]

In the chapter headed "Freemen Need no Guardians" Wilson demonstrates the fusion of traditional Jeffersonian concepts of government with his concept of the New Freedom. Government cannot be entrusted to any special class, he insists, whether it be entrusted to the special interests of the traditional Hamiltonians or the trustees of either the great concentrations of power and wealth or the governmental trustees of Roosevelt's New Nationalism. "I believe, as I believe in nothing else, in the average integrity and the average intelligence of the American people, and I do not believe that the intelligence of America can be put into commission anywhere," he writes; no man or group of men can be entrusted with the freedom of the American people.

In turning to specific provisions of the New Freedom, Wilson insists that its farm policy is to free the farmer, whose work is the foundation of a free society, from the domination of special interests; in discusing the tariff, his traditional Democratic rejection of the protective tariff is buttressed with his insistence that a free economy in a free society needs no support from artificial—and corrupting—restraints of trade. In discussing the government itself, and specifically the Congress as well as the business empires, Wilson insists that the people will demand a new openness in conducting business that is essentially that of the people. "Permit me to mix a few metaphors," Wilson writes; "they [the people] are going to open doors; they are going to let up blinds; they are going to drag sick things out into the open air and into the light of the sun";[12] "the so-called radicalism of our times," he writes, "is simply the effort of nature to release the generous energies of our people."[13] And that can only be true when the truth is no longer hidden from them.

However, Wilson's most obvious and pointed rejection of Roosevelt's New Nationalism lies in his attitude toward the trusts. Whereas Roosevelt would distinguish between good and bad trusts and have government act accordingly, Wilson does not; "private monopoly is indefensible and intolerable,"[14] he insists; it is evil by its very nature and evil can be neither tolerated nor excused. The handful of willful men who control the raw materials and the means of production also control the nation, by sheer power if not by default, and, Wilson insists, that cannot be tolerated.

Essentially, to Wilson, the path to the New Freedom is both simple and obvious: we have but to begin, to find a new equilibrium for this new age, in essence, a new definition of freedom; in the new age, Wilson says, "human freedom consists in perfect adjustments of human interests and human activities and human energies," and this is the alignment that his policies are designed to bring about.

The New Freedom, as Wilson defined it and attempted to bring it into existence, was not only traditional in its attempt to return to simpler relationships; it was entirely a domestic program, related only to the internal functioning of the nation. Shortly before going to Washington, he remarked to his friend E. G. Conklin of Princeton that "it would be the irony of fate if my administration had to deal chiefly with foreign affairs" (Baker, IV, 55); he felt that he was badly prepared in foreign affairs—indeed he virtually ignored them during the campaign—and his earlier comments suggested an uncritical acceptance of the concepts of manifest destiny and the new American imperialism. His interests were in domestic affairs, his academic career had been built largely upon his examination of the inner workings of government, and his programs were based upon traditional American ideals and programs. Furthermore, he had always been interested in the construction of constitutions—of balanced laws by which men might live together in peace for their collective well-being. All this he planned to use for the benefit of the American people.

II   First Inaugural Address

In his inaugural address on March 4, 1913, one of the few truly great presidential inaugural addresses in American history, Wilson made clear his preoccupation with domestic affairs. In it he emphasizes the American potential for greatness and goodness; the areas in which the reality has failed to achieve its potential; and the path by which the two may be brought together. His tone is optimistic and confident as he defines the potential:

We have been refreshed by a new insight into our own life.

We see that in many things that life is very great. It is incomparably great in its material aspects, in its body of wealth, in the diversity and sweep of its energy, in the industries which have been conceived and built up by the genius of individual men and the limitless enterprise of groups of men. It is great, also, in its moral force.

Nowhere else in the world have noble men and women exhibited in more striking forms the beauty and the energy of sympathy and helpfulness and counsel in their efforts to rectify wrong, alleviate suffering, and set the weak in the way of strength and hope. We have built up, moreover a great system of government. . . . Our life contains every great thing and contains it in rich abundance.

But the evil has come with the good, and much fine gold has been corroded. With riches has come inexcusable waste. . . . We have been proud of our industrial achievements, but we have not hitherto stopped thoughtfully enough to count the human cost, the cost of lives snuffed out, of energies overtaxed and broken. . . . The great government we loved has been made use of for private and selfish purposes, and those who used it had forgotten the people. (Baker-Dodd II, I, 1–3)

The items which Wilson listed as the basis for his "work of restoration" were perhaps predictable: the removal of tariff restrictions on trade; a revamped banking and currency system under federal control; agricultural support; conservation and health services; sanitary laws; and laws controlling the conditions of labor "which individuals are powerless to determine for themselves," all of this to be accomplished at the same time that personal freedom and property rights are safeguarded.

Yet in phraseology reminiscent of his critique of those who reject "mere literature," who emphasize scientific methods at the cost of human values, Wilson insists that this progressive reform "will be no cool process of mere science" but rather "like some air out of God's own presence" (Baker Dodd II, I, 5), dominated by humane values and high purpose. He concludes:

This is not a day of triumph; it is a day of dedication. Here muster, not the forces of party, but the forces of humanity. Men's hearts wait upon us; men's lives hang in the balance; men's hopes call upon us to say what we will do. Who shall live up to the great trust? Who dares fail to try? I summon all honest men, all patriotic, all forward-looking men, to my side. God helping me, I will not fail them if they will but counsel and sustain me! (Baker-Dodd II, I, 5–6)

Whether Wilson's prgressivism was shallow and superficial as some critics have insisted[15] or profound and far-reaching, as others maintain, it was real, and Wilson was determined that policy should become legislative fact. Wilson had achieved the Presidency free of bargains, commitments, or concessions, and he was free to make of it what he would. At the same time, however, he was determined that the new society be based upon Democratic tradition: low tariffs, currency reform, and agricultural support. But he would take it forward into new areas: regulation of working conditions for men and the protection of women and children from exploitation.

The history of the New Freedom, of its successes, its failures, its limited achievements, and the ultimate irony of its being swept up in the international trauma no man could foresee or control are properly in the province of political and social history rather than that of literature. But in the process Wilson's Progressive program was marked by a series of documents, less "literary" perhaps than those of his academic years and yet more forceful, more direct, and consequently more immediately effective as well as more rhetorically eloquent than his parallel writings from the past.

III   *Message to Congress*

Almost immediately after his inauguration Wilson began to reshape the Presidency into his own idea of what it should be. Perhaps his most abrupt change from tradition was his message to a special session of Congress on the tariff, which he delivered in person on April 8, 1913. Since Jefferson's administration, Presidential messages had been sent to Congress, to be read by a clerk. But Wilson, perhaps as a remnant of his old interest in the prime-ministerial form of governmental leadership, had determined that he was to be the leader of his party and the leader of the nation. Consequently, from the very beginning he determined that the Presidency must not be held aloof from the legislative branch, but must provide its leadership. Not only did Wilson continue to address Congress in person upon measures of importance, as he did until his illness made it impossible, but he also gave the Presidency a new role and a new visibility that continues to the present, a role that does provide for legislative leadership and Presidential responsibility for legislation passed. Such an arrangement placed a major premium on party loyalty that also continues today.

Wilson's address to the Congress was short and pointed, and his opening statement makes clear the fact that his purpose was not merely tariff reductions but a declaration of common purpose and an assumption of leadership:

I am very glad indeed to have this opportunity to address the Two Houses directly and to verify for myself the impression that the President of the United States is a person, not a mere department of the Government hailing Congress from some isolated island of jealous power, sending messages, not speaking naturally and with his own voice—that he is a human being trying to cooperate with other human beings in a common service. After this pleasant experience I shall feel quite normal in all our dealings with one another. (Baker-Dodd II, I, 32)

Almost immediately, however, Wilson makes it clear that his purpose is not to engage in discussion or debate, but to inform his audience what they must do:

We must abolish everything that bears even the semblance of privilege or of any kind of artificial advantage, and put our business men and producers under the stimulation of a constant necessity to be efficient, economical, and enterprising, masters of competitive supremacy, better workers and merchants than any in the world. Aside from the duties laid upon articles which we do not, and probably can not, produce, therefore, and the duties laid upon luxuries and merely for the sake of the revenues they yield, the object of the tariff duties henceforth laid must be effective competition, the whetting of American wits by contest with the wits of the rest of the world. (Baker-Dodd II, I, 33–34)

With his proposed tariff revision very clearly a part—the first part—of his New Freedom for Americans, Wilson points out that other parts, essentially those that he had defined in his campaign speeches, will follow:

It is best, indeed it is necessary, to begin with the tariff. I will urge nothing upon you now at the opening of your session which can obscure that first object or divert our energies from that clearly defined duty. At a later time I may take the liberty of calling your attention to reforms which should press close upon the heels of the tariff changes, if not accompany them, of which the chief is the reform of our banking and currency laws; but just now I refrain. For the present, I put these matters on one side and think only of this one thing—of the changes in our fiscal system which may best serve to open once more the free channels of prosperity to a great people whom we would serve to the utmost and throughout both rank and file.

I sincerely thank you for your courtesy. (Baker-Dodd II, I, 35)

In this address not only is the nature of Wilson's relationship with Congress made clear as he saw that it must be, but the pattern of his future communications is made equally clear, very much in the manner of a schoolmaster giving an assignment to his students. There is no condescension but a deep respect that nevertheless makes clear the relative positions of the two parties to the relationship; the broader context of the issue is described in general terms; the specific task is defined, clearly but succinctly; then the relationship of this specific task to future problems is made clear. So much so did this pattern become the basis of Wilson's Presidential message to Congress that it even served as the basis of the later, longer, more detailed request for a declaration of war against the Imperial German Government.

Wilson's emphasis upon his campaign-promised reforms continued. On June 23, 1913, he again appeared before a joint session of Congress, speaking this time on his demand for a new banking and currency law. Again the tenor of his argument was based upon his search for "the New Freedom": "It is absolutely imperative that we give the business men of this country a banking and currency system by means of which they can make use of the freedom of enterprise and of individual initiative which we are about to bestow upon them" (Baker-Dodd II, I, 37). Perhaps most important from the point of view of democratic tradition was Wilson's demand that currency-control reform resume at the point at which it had been discontinued in the Jackson era: "the control of the system of banking and of issue which our new laws are to set up must be public, not private, must be vested in the Government itself, so that the banks may be the instruments, not the masters, of business and of individual enterprise and initiative" (Baker-Dodd II, I, 39–40).

By the end of 1913, as he again broke tradition by delivering his first annual message to Congress in person, Wilson had won substantial victories in both areas of reform, and a third major program, antitrust regulation, remained, together with the lesser need to enact legislation for making credit easier for farmers. Both of these recommended programs received a good deal of Wilson's attention in his State of the Union message on December 2, but they were not the only measures on his reform program. Matters for future attention included America's new empire abroad:

. . . Porto Rico, Hawaii are ours, indeed, but not ours to do what we please with. Such territories, once regarded as mere possessions, are no longer to be selfishly exploited; they are part of the domain of public conscience and of serviceable and enlightened statesmanship. We must administer them for the people who live in them and with the same sense of responsibility to them as toward our own people in our domestic affairs. . . . (Baker-Dodd II, I 76–77)

Wilson's attitude toward Hawaii and Puerto Rico was perhaps predictable: "giving them the ample and familiar rights and privileges accorded our own citizens . . . but in the Philippines we must go further" (Baker-Dodd II, I, 77). To Wilson, as to the antiimperialist element among the Progressives, only carefully prepared independence could suffice.

Wilson listed other goals: mine-control reform, railroad employees' protection; international agreement. In his conclusion, Wilson was both pleased with his relationship with Congress and optimistic of good future relations and continued Progressive legislation. Only one shadow obscured America's future as Wilson saw it at the time, and that was abroad, to the South: "There can be no certain prospect of peace in America until General Huerta has surrendered his usurped authority in Mexico. . . . We shall not, I believe, be obliged to alter our policy of watchful waiting" (Baker-Dodd II, I, 71–72).

During 1914 Wilson continued his personal leadership of Congress, appearing again on January 20 to present his request for antitrust legislation, and again on April 14, to deliver his message on the Mexican situation. By early fall his major legislative program was essentially complete. On September 26, he signed the Federal Trade Act, which was to regulate interstate commerce, and on October 15 he signed the Clayton Anti-Trust Act. Together with his tariff bill and the Federal Reserve Act, he had accomplished much of his initial program, and his reform program had become reality. But during 1914 personal and public tragedy combined to prevent much of the sense of accomplishment that he might otherwise have felt. On August 6, his wife, Ellen Axson Wilson, died, after a period of increasingly serious illness, and earlier that same month, world war had erupted in Europe. In the former tragedy, Wilson was heard by his physician to cry out, "Oh my God, what am I going to do?" and later, "Leave me alone. I want to think." But he was remarried sixteen months later to Edith Bolling Galt, an attractive Washington widow.

In the latter case, however, Wilson proceeded cautiously but confidently, immediately declaring American neutrality. He had continued a confident Mexican policy, had moved with equal confidence in the Colorado coal strike, and had written a major description of his "Democratic Foreign Policy" in the *World's Work* for October 1914.

As 1914 came to a close, Wilson faced new problems: Mexico, the war, the loss of much of his Democratic margin in the House. As he told Josephus Daniels, "Every reform we have won will be lost if we go into this war. We have been making a fight on special privilege. We have got new tariff and currency and trust legislation. We don't know yet how they will work. They are not thoroughly set" (Baker V, 77).

Nevertheless, as he looked back upon the past two years, he was pleased. Writing to William G. McAdoo, he said, "Ten or twelve years ago the country was torn and excited by an agitation which shook the foundations of her political life" (Baker-Dodd II, I, 211), but that time had passed, and the American Progressive future seemed secure.

If the Wilson administration had ended at this point, or even two years later, it would have been characterized historically as a moderate success, with perhaps its most significant and lasting accomplishment not the Progressive legislation of which Wilson was so proud but the new dimension he had added to the institution of the Presidency. In his second annual address to Congress on December 8, 1914, he reviewed the record, concluding that "Our program of legislation with regard to business is now virtually complete" (Baker-Dodd II, I, 215). But at the same time the shadows of the future, those that would elevate a moderately successful President to greatness, received passing attention as he asked for a measure of preparedness. But the real challenge, he insisted, was at home.

CHAPTER 9

The President, the War, and the World

NEITHER Woodrow Wilson nor his Secretary of State, William Jennings Bryan, were pacifists—Wilson had supported the Spanish-American War and Bryan had briefly served as colonel of a Nebraska volunteer infantry regiment, although the Republican McKinley administration had carefully kept his regiment in the United States—but both men abhorred violence and both were strong moralists. At the same time, both men were relatively unskilled and uninterested in foreign affairs, and, in the American nineteenth-century tradition, both men were convinced that America's destiny was essentially domestic.

However, Wilson and Bryan were fundamentally different in their exercise of morality; Wilson determined never to compromise moral principle, and Bryan equally determined that practical politics at times demand compromise. As the course of world events during 1915 and 1916 moved America closer to participation in the war, it was evident that the two would split over the proper means of remaining neutral and at peace, although they agreed almost wholeheartedly upon domestic policy and the basic issues of peace and progress in the campaign of 1916. Ironically, however, when Bryan left the cabinet, it was because neither of them would compromise moral principle, although they parted on good terms.

During the last two years of Wilson's first term, foreign affairs increasingly took precedence over domestic affairs, first shaping them and then for all practical purposes replacing them, even to the extent that "Peace"—a reflection of foreign affairs—led "Prosperity" in the Democratic campaign slogan for 1916. However, even while chaotic conditions in Mexico and problems stemming from the European war made increasing demands upon Wilson's attention, nevertheless, the age of reform was not only not over but he had to act judiciously when antiliberal legislation threatened. On January 28,

127

1915, forced to veto the first Immigration Bill, Wilson made clear both his reluctance to veto and at the same time his determination to do so:

> It is with deep regret that I find myself constrained by clear conviction to return this bill (H. R. 6060, "An act to regulate the immigration of aliens to and the residence of aliens in the United States") without my signature. Not only do I feel it to be a very serious matter to exercise the power of veto in any case, because it involves opposing the single judgment of the President to the judgment of a majority of both the Houses of Congress, a step which no man who realizes his own liability to error can take without great hesitation, but also because this particular bill is in so many important respects admirable, well conceived, and desirable. . . . (Baker-Dodd II, I, 252)

Wilson's humility, so evident in his opening lines, departs very quickly, however, as Wilson, the lecturer, proceeds to give the Congress a fundamental lesson in the nature of the American tradition:

> In two particulars of vital consequence this bill embodies a radical departure from the traditional and long-established policy of this country, a policy in which our people have conceived the very character of their Government to be expressed, the very mission and spirit of the Nation in respect of its relations to the peoples of the world. . . . It seeks to all but close entirely the gates of asylum which have always been open to those who could find nowhere else the right and opportunity of constitutional agitation for what they conceived to be the natural and inalienable rights of men. . . .
>
> Restrictions like these, adopted earlier in our history as a Nation, would very materially have altered the course and cooled the humane ardors of our politics. The right of political asylum has brought to this country many a man of noble character. . . . It is difficult for me to believe that the full effect of this feature of the bill was realized when it was framed and adopted, and it is impossible for me to assent to it in the form in which it is cast. (Baker-Dodd II, I, 252–53)

The most objectionable features of the bill were to Wilson its literacy tests and other tests and restrictions that were designed for "restriction, not selection" (Baker-Dodd II, I, 254) of immigrants, particularly eliminating those who lacked opportunity while admitting those who have already known it, in effect reversing the traditional American attitude toward the world's unfortunates. Then, in a conclusion that returns to his initial tone of mock humility after his very forceful and pointed lecture, Wilson concludes ironically: "I have no foolish pride of opinion in this question. I am not foolish enough to profess to know the wishes and ideals of America better than the body of her chosen representatives know them. I only want instruction direct from those whose fortunes, with ours and all men's, are involved" (Baker-Dodd II, I, 254).

It is unfortunate that this, one of Wilson's strongest messages to Congress, certainly the strongest of his first administration, has been misinterpreted by those scholars who fail to perceive the strong note of mock humility with which Wilson begins and ends the message, and, in particular, the irony of Wilson, the historian, the professor, and the President seeking instruction that would lead him to reverse his strongly expressed opinions and his determination to teach Congress something about American tradition. It was not an invitation for continued agitation, as John Morton Blum insists;[1] it was a clear statement of position by a man whose mother was herself an immigrant. When a similar bill was passed in 1917, Wilson's veto was equally powerful, but the second bill, in the early days of his second administration, was passed over his veto. If the Congress was willing to close the doors of America, the President certainly was not. However, no President has more clearly expressed the democratic ideal than Wilson in his second veto, when he wrote, "Tests of quality and of purpose cannot be objected to on principle, but tests of opportunity surely may be" (Baker-Dodd II, I, 420).

I *Mexican Policy*

If Wilson's record of Progressive aims and achievements in his first administration were clear and successful, his policy toward Mexico certainly was neither. Early in his first administration he had begun a policy of bypassing the regular State Department and other governmental structures by sending a personal friend, Henry Jones Ford, to the Philippines to make a confidential report of conditions. So pleased was he with Ford's elaborate report that he sent William Bayard Hale and John Lind on similar missions to Mexico, just as in December 1914 he had sent Colonel Edward M. House to Germany and England. Hale, Wilson's campaign biographer, and Lind, a friend of Bryan and an anti-Catholic, were poor choices; not only did they come into conflict with the American ambassador, Henry Lane Wilson, but their reports were ambiguous and opinionated, thus further obscuring a situation in which Wilson had little factual information but a determination to teach the Mexicans—and later the Haitians, Nicaraguans, and Dominicans—to construct democratic governments and elect virtuous men.

Wilson's initial refusal to recognize the Victoriano Huerta government, his insistence upon constitutional elections, his seizure of Vera Cruz, his attempts at settlement through the agency of Argentina, Brazil, and Chile, his reaction to the Pancho Villa insurgency, initially supporting it and then after Villa's raid on Columbus, New Mexico, sending into Mexico the punitive expedition under Brigadier General John J. Pershing, the confused combat that led Wilson nearly to war, the unsuccessful negotiating committee, and the recognition of the revolutionary government of Venustiano Carranza, were all elements of a policy based on good will and ignorance, further complicated by a search for order in a situation more whimsical, perhaps even more Quixotic, than Wilson was capable of recognizing.

II *The Movement toward War*

With the withdrawal of Pershing's troops on February 4, 1917, Wilson's Mexican diplomatic venture was over. But in the heat of the campaign of the fall of 1916 and with the increasingly complex effects of the European war on American neutrality, the failure to find a workable Mexican policy was largely overlooked. The Wilson-Bryan policy toward the war was based on two principles: a strict neutrality and a reaffirmation of the American right of freedom of the sea and freedom to travel. Inevitably the nature of the war brought the first into question; the second element took Americans into the war zone; and the issue of preparedness for a war that seemed increasingly probable led to strained relations abroad and at home. Finally the two men disagreed, Bryan resigning over Wilson's firmness that, Bryan was convinced, could only lead America to war.

As he sought to bring some measure of stability to the increasingly threatening European situation, Wilson made his position—and America's position as he saw it—clear on a number of occasions, often seeking speaking engagements at which he might make major position statements. Thus, in an address to the Daughters of the American Revolution on April 19, 1915, he used the opportunity to define true neutrality as America must practice it:

We cannot afford to sympathize with anybody or anything except the passing generation of human beings. America forgets what she was born for when she does exactly the way every other nation does—when she loses her recollection of her main object, as sometimes nations do and sometimes perhaps she had done, in pursuing some immediate and transitory object. . . .

We must preserve the judicial temperament, not because we would sit in judgment upon others, but because we should ultimately wish to sit in judgment upon ourselves, because we should ultimately wish to be justified by our own consciences and by the standards of our national life. . . .
(Baker-Dodd II, I, 300–310)

A month later, in addressing several thousand foreign-born American citizens in Philadelphia, Wilson went beyond this essentially moralistic and idealistic definition in a speech that became perhaps the most widely quoted, praised, and—particularly by Theodore Roosevelt— condemned of his Presidency:

America must have this consciousness, that on all sides it touches elbows and touches hearts with all the nations of mankind. The example of America must be a special example. The example of America must be the example not merely of peace because it will not fight, but of peace because peace is the healing and elevating influence of the world and strife is not. There is such a thing as a man being too proud to fight. There is such a thing as a nation being so right that it does not need to convince others by force that it is right. . . .
(Baker-Dodd II, I, 331)

During 1916 Wilson began to make tentative suggestions about a plan for the postwar world that would not only justify America's aloof righteousness but that could only be advanced and carried through to a successful conclusion by a nation that had refused to be corrupted by national greed or international violence. This plan, to which he committed both himself and the nation, was for a league of nations. He first mentioned it publicly in a speech before the League to Enforce Peace, in Washington on May 27, 1916. In the speech he first made clear the lessons of the war, that

the principle of public right must henceforth take precedence over the individual interests of particular nations, and that the nations of the world must in some way band themselves together to see that that right prevails as against any sort of selfish aggression; that henceforth alliance must not be set up against alliance, understanding against understanding, but that there must be a common agreement for a common object, and that at the heart of that common object must lie the inviolable rights of peoples and of mankind . . . it is imperative that they should agree to co-operate in a common cause, and that they should so act that the guiding principle of that common cause shall be even-handed and impartial justice. . . . (Baker-Dodd II, II, 186–87)

In the same speech Wilson pledged as an article of public as well as personal faith the ideas that later became the foundation of both his Fourteen Points and the American position at the Peace Conference:

We believe these fundamental things: First, that every people has a right to choose the sovereignty under which they shall live. . . . Second, that the small states of the world have a right to enjoy the same respect for their sovereignty and for their territorial integrity that the great and powerful nations insist upon. And, third, that the world has a right to be free from every disturbance of its peace that has its origin in aggression and disregard of the rights of peoples and nations. . . .
There is nothing that the United States wants for itself that any other nation has. . . . (Baker-Dodd II, II, 187)

During the Presidential campaign that fall Wilson returned to his pledge of an American role in making a permanent peace in the postwar world. On October 12, 1916, in Indianapolis, he said:

I have said, and shall say again, that when the great present war is over it will be the duty of America to join with the other nations of the world in some kind of league for the maintenance of peace. . . . America shall not stand for national aggression, but shall stand for the just conceptions and bases of peace, for the competitions of merit alone, and for the generous rivalry of liberty. . . . (Baker-Dodd II, II, 360–61)

In 1916 Wilson saw his increased emphasis upon preparedness lead to legislation authorizing the doubling of the size of the regular army, increasing the authority of the War Department, and providing for construction of a navy second to none. But as the campaign approached, the Roosevelt Progressives returned to the Republican party, which nominated Charles Evans Hughes, a moderate. With Bryan's support, Wilson became the champion of progressivism and peace. With support from liberals—for example, Jane Addams, who had been influential in writing the Progressive party platform in 1912, John Reed, Ray Stannard Baker, Walter Lippmann, Herbert Croly, and dozens more, most of whom had supported Roosevelt in 1912—labor, including the railroad unions, and farmers West and

South, he forged an alliance dedicated to "Peace and Prosperity." But already it was evident that continued peace was perhaps more elusive than ever before. Even Wilson, in a speech at Cincinnati on October 26, made clear what he saw as the shadow of the future:

I believe that the business of neutrality is over; not because I want it to be over but I mean this, that war now has such a scale that the position of neutrals sooner or later becomes intolerable. . . .

We must have a society of nations. . . . The nations of the world must get together and say, "Nobody can hereafter be neutral as respects the disturbance of the world's peace. . . ." (Baker Dodd II, II, 381)

III *The Second Inaugural Address*

Reelected in November, his attention focused almost entirely upon increasingly difficult relations with Germany—although on December 12 Germany had announced its willingness to meet the allies at a conference table, on February 1 she resumed unrestricted submarine warfare—Wilson nevertheless was unwilling to give up entirely his dream of peace. On February 26 he asked Congress for authority to arm merchant ships, and on March 5 he took his second oath of office. In an inaugural address remarkably different from its predecessor four years before, Wilson defined the elements of what had become not merely a foreign policy but a policy for human survival:

. . . We are provincials no longer. The tragical events of the thirty months of vital turmoil through which we have just passed have made us citizens of the world. There can be no turning back. Our own fortunes as a nation are involved, whether we would have it so or not. . . .

And it is imperative that we should stand together. We are being forged into a new unity amidst the fires that now blaze throughout the world. In their ardent heart we shall, in God's providence, let us hope, be purged of faction and division, purified of the errant humors of party and of private interest, and shall stand forth in the days to come with a new dignity of national pride and spirit. Let each man see to it that the dedication in his own heart, the high purpose of the Nation in his own mind, ruler of his own will and desire. . . . (Baker-Dodd III, 1, 3–4)

In tones not unlike Abraham Lincoln's call for a national dedication nearly fifty-four years before, Wilson had not only made clear to the nation the price of liberty, but he made clear too the fact that he was

willing to pay that price or more. Then, in conclusion, he looked
beyond the moment:

. . . The shadows that now lie dark upon our path will soon be dispelled and
we shall walk with the light all about us if we be but true to ourselves,—to
ourselves as we have wished to be known in the counsels of the world and in
the thought of all those who love liberty and justice and the right exalted.
(Baker-Dodd III, 1, 5)

IV   *The Declaration of War*

At this point, on the verge of war the outcome of which was beyond
his ability to predict, Wilson became more eloquent than he had ever
been before as he attempted to convey the sense of what he saw as the
travail through which the American people had to pass like John
Christian before they could find national, indeed, human fulfillment.
As he stood there on the inaugural platform, the nation had less than a
month of uncertain peace left. On April 2, 1917, he appeared before a
joint session of Congress to request a declaration of war. Again, with a
clear image of the solemnity of the occasion, he looked beyond it,
describing the meaning of the war in a sentence that became a slogan:

. . . We are glad, now that we see the facts with no veil of false pretense about
them, to fight thus for the ultimate peace of the world and for the liberation of
its peoples, the German peoples included: for the rights of nations great and
small and the privilege of men everywhere to choose their way of life and of
obedience. The world must be made safe for democracy. Its peace must be
planted upon the tested foundations of political liberty. We have no selfish
ends to serve. We desire no conquest, no dominion. We seek no indemnities
for ourselves, no material compensation for the sacrifices we shall freely
make. We are but one of the champions of the rights of mankind. We shall be
satisfied when those rights have been made as secure as the faith and the
freedom of nations can make them. (Baker-Dodd III, I, 14)

With the war the reality with which Wilson was to live for the next
year and a half and the vision of the postwar world the increasingly
elusive ideal that he was to seek for the rest of his life, indeed for
which he was to sacrifice his health and perhaps his life, Wilson
embarked on the great crusade of his life, that which would ultimately
proclaim a new freedom not only for America but for the world.
Nevertheless, in spite of the demands of war he did not lose sight
entirely of the need for continued reform at home; on March 2, 1917,

he had signed the Organic Act for Puerto Rico, making that island an American territory and its inhabitants American citizens. On October 25, 1917, he declared his support for women's suffrage; on September 30, 1918, he addressed the Senate in an appeal for the passage of the nineteenth amendment, and on June 30, 1920, he appealed to Tennessee to become the thirty-sixth state to ratify it, so that it might become law.

V   The Fourteen Points

During the years of the war itself Wilson continued to examine the nature and conditions of peace, combining them in an address to a joint session of Congress on January 18, 1918. In what was undoubtedly the most significant, coherent, and idealistic document that was produced on either side during the war, Wilson defined what became known as his Fourteen Points:

. . . The program of the world's peace, therefore, is our program; and that program, the only possible program, as we see it, is this:

I. Open covenants of peace, openly arrived at, after which there shall be no private international understandings of any kind but diplomacy shall proceed always frankly and in the public view.

II. Absolute freedom of navigation upon the seas. . . .

III. The removal, so far as possible, of all economic barriers and the establishment of an equality of trade conditions. . . .

IV. Adequate guarantees given and taken that national armaments will be reduced to the lowest point consistent with domestic safety.

V. A free, open-minded, and absolutely impartial adjustment of all colonial claims, based upon a strict observance of the principle that in determining all such questions of sovereignty the interests of the populations concerned must have equal weight. . . .

VI. The evacuation of all Russian territory and . . . an unhampered and unembarrassed opportunity for the independent determination of her own political development. . . .

VII. Belgium . . . must be evacuated and restored. . . .

VIII. All French territory should be freed and the invaded portions restored. . . .

IX. A readjustment of the frontiers of Italy . . . along clearly recognizable lines of nationality.

X. The peoples of Austria-Hungary . . . should be accorded the freest opportunity of autonomous development.

XI. Rumania, Serbia, and Montenegro should be evacuated; . . . Serbia accorded free and secure access to the sea. . . .

XII. The Turkish portions of the present Ottoman Empire should be assured a secure sovereignty, but the other nationalities . . . should be assured an . . . unmolested opportunity of autonomous development; and the Dardanelles should be permanently opened as a free passage. . . .

XIII. An independent Polish state should be erected. . . .

XIV. A general association of nations must be formed under specific covenants for the purpose of affording mutual guarantees of political independence and territorial integrity to great and small states alike. . . . (Baker-Dodd III, I, 159–61)

Wilson's fourteen points have been and will continue to be criticized for a great many reasons, among them the failure to recognize the essential ambiguity of national states and political alignments, the attempt to reduce European complexities that have stood for centuries to a handful of declarations, the promising of solutions impossible to achieve, the arrogance of a man who would reorder the world. All these criticisms and more have some validity, just as it is always possible to take exceptions to any other grand plan or idealistic pronouncement. Yet the Fourteen Points were Wilson at his most idealistic and realistic at once. In essence, he had demonstrated once again his belief that man had the potential for constructing an orderly, meaningful, and fulfilling environment if he had the will and the moral strength and determination to do it. Often, to Wilson, this meant the rational examination and reordering of man's institutions; always it meant open, honest, complete discussion and debate, with the kind of honesty and disregard for fears and ambitions that limit men, distort their ideals, or corrupt their souls.

The determination with which Wilson pursued his ideal world was emphasized numerous times during the war. On July 4, 1918, at Mount Vernon, he not only simplified his plan for peace but made clear the attitude toward it that was later to confound not only his political enemies but many of his supporters as well:

. . . The Past and the Present are in deadly grapple and the peoples of the world are being done to death between them.

There can be but one issue. The settlement must be final. There can be no compromise. No halfway decision would be tolerable. No halfway decision is conceivable. These are the ends for which the associated peoples of the world are fighting and which must be conceded them before there can be peace:

I. The destruction of every arbitrary power anywhere that can separately, secretly, and of its single choice disturb the peace of the world. . . .

II. The settlement of every question . . . upon the basis of the free acceptance of that settlement by the people immediately conceived. . . .

III. The consent of all nations to be governed in their conduct toward each other by . . . principles of honor and of respect for the common law of civilized society . . . no private plots or conspiracies hatched, no selfish injuries wrought. . . .

IV. The establishment of an organization of peace. . . . (Baker-Dodd III, I, 233–34)

Not only did Wilson see this program as absolutely necessary for peace, but he saw it equally necessary for human liberation, for a process that had begun in war nearly a century and a half before:

. . . Here were started forces which the great nation against which they were primarily directed at first regarded as a revolt against its rightful authority but which it has long since seen to have been a step in the liberation of its own people as well as of the people of the United States; and I stand here now to speak,—speak proudly and with confident hope,—of the spread of this revolt, this liberation, to the great stage of the world itself. . . ! (Baker-Dodd III, I, 234–35)

Even as he spoke the end of the war was in sight; American troops were taking over increasingly greater segments of the Western front; the Second Battle of the Marne had halted Germany's last great offensive; Bulgaria had surrendered; and on October 6 a new German government requested an armistice to pursue peace based upon Wilson's Fourteen Points.

Yet the war went on, as did its breakup: mutiny in the German fleet on November 3, the Austrian surrender on November 4, and, in the midst of American mid-term elections that lost Democratic control of both houses of Congress, the emergence of rumors and feelers that led to the Armistice on November 11. Almost immediately Wilson determined to go to Europe, to insure personally that the peace would be permanent. Still convinced of the power of personal persuasion, determined to carry his concept of the New Freedom to the peoples of the world, Wilson was prepared to break another precedent—that of the President's traditional refusal to leave American soil—in order to establish yet another, that of the President as negotiator, just as he had established a direct, personal presence of the President in the halls of Congress.

On December 2, 1918, less than a month after the Armistice, Wilson delivered his annual message to Congress on the state of the nation. In a speech more deeply felt, more low-keyed and humble, and at the same time more eloquent than Wilson had ever given before Congress, he marked the end of the war, the beginning of peace, and the work that remained. First, however, Wilson spoke as an historian, withholding judgment on the events of the immediate past:

> The year that has elasped . . . has been so crowded with great events, great processes, and great results that I cannot hope to give you an adequate picture of its transactions or of the far-reaching changes which have been wrought in the life of our nation and the world. You have yourselves witnessed these things, as I have. It is too soon to assess them; and we who stand in the midst of them and are part of them are less qualified than men of another generation will be to say what they mean or even what they have been. But some great outstanding facts are unmistakable. . . . (Baker-Dodd III, I, 308)

The facts Wilson recounts are both statistical and remarkable: the movement of great armies abroad; the courage of American soldiers; the victories; the national spirit; the contributions of women. Here, too, Wilson insists that the franchise is their just due: "The least tribute we can pay them is to make them the equals of men in political rights as they have proved themselves their equals in every field of practical work they have entered, whether for themselves or for their country" (Baker-Dodd III, I, 311).

He goes on, then, to mark the peace and the future:

> And now we are sure of the great triumph for which every sacrifice was made. It has come, come in its completeness, and with the pride and inspiration of these days of achievement quick within us we turn to the tasks of peace again,—a peace secure against the violence of irresponsible monarchs and ambitious military coteries and made ready for a new order, for new foundations of justice and fair dealing.
>
> We are about to give order and organization to this peace not only for ourselves, but for the other peoples of the world as well. . . . (Baker-Dodd III, I, 312)

VI *The Search for Peace*

Many accounts have been written of Wilson's two trips to Europe during 1919 in search of peace, and nearly as many interpretations as accounts exist. His reception by the peoples of Europe, those who had heard the message of the Fourteen Points, who had captured something of the visionary future that he described, was magnificent;

his reception by heads of state was more restrained. On Janurary 18, 1919, he opened the Peace Conference:

. . . we are trusted to do a great thing, to do it in the highest spirit of friendship and accommodation, and to do it as promptly as possible, in order that the hearts of men may have fear lifted from them and that they may return to those pursuits of life which will bring them happiness and contentment and prosperity. . . . (Baker-Dodd III, I 391)

Upon his return from the first session of the Peace Conference, Wilson knew that the outcome, still inconclusive, was going to be perhaps less sweeping and less satisfactory, but in a meeting at the Metropolitan Opera in New York, speaking on the same platform with former President William Howard Taft, who had endorsed the League of Nations, Wilson spoke confidently of America and the League: "An overwhelming majority of the American people is in favor of the League of Nations. I know that that is true. I have had unmistakable intimations of it from every part of the country. . . " (Baker-Dodd III, I, 444).

In his concluding words, in this speech on the eve of his return to France, he re-created the hope of the people of Europe:

When I was in Italy, a little limping group of Italian soldiers sought an interview with me. I could not conjecture what it was they were going to say to me, and with the greatest simplicity, with touching simplicity, they presented me with a petition in favor of the League of Nations.

Their wounded limbs, their impaired vitality, were the only argument they brought with them. It was a simple request that I lend all the influence I might happen to have to relieve future generations of the sacrifices they had been obliged to make. . . .

It is inconceivable that we should disappoint them, and we shall not. . . . (Baker-Dodd III, I, 454–55)

The second session of the conference was stormy; at one point he threatened to leave as disagreements increased and the European demands for a conventional punitive treaty predominated. Ill with what was diagnosed as influenza but which was apparently a stroke, quarreling strenuously with Italian demands which he saw as contrary to the right of self-determination of peoples, he carried on, and on June 28, he signed the treaty for the United States and carried it home for ratification, dissatisfied with much of it but confident because it included a League of Nations, the means by which old wrongs and new might be righted and the future of the world made secure. On July 10 he presented the treaty to the Senate:

The stage is set, the destiny disclosed. It has come about by no plan of our conceiving, but by the hand of God who led us into this way. We cannot turn back. We can only go forward, with lifted eyes and freshened spirit, to follow the vision. It was of this that we dreamed at our birth. America shall in truth show the way. The light streams upon the path ahead, and nowhere else. (Baker-Dodd III, I 551–52)

VII *The Fight for the League*

This was perhaps the greatest moment of Wilson's life; it was certainly his last triumphant moment. The Senate that he addressed was not that of six years before; Senator William E. Borah of Idaho declared the treaty totally unacceptable with American participation in the League a part of it; other Republicans demanded "mild" reservations; Senator Henry Cabot Lodge and others accepted the "idea" of a League but rejected its present form, demanding "strong" reservations. Differences quickly became political warfare, with compromises an impossibility as Wilson determined to fight his opponents, with Lodge at their head. Perhaps recognizing that enough injustice remained in the treaty to make another war inevitable unless the League, as it was constructed, became a reality, certainly confident of the rightness of his cause, neither a compromiser by nature nor tolerant of evil, certain of his support by the majority of Americans, Wilson and his opponents took the case to the people.

Still not completely recovered from his stroke, struggling with the domestic issues that demanded increasing attention in a return to peace—inflation, reconversion, labor problems, demobilization of men and industry—tired, Wilson set out on September 3 on a national speaking tour to marshal the support of the people. He planned to visit every state west of the Mississippi in a twenty-seven-day whistlestop tour, returning to Washington at the end of the month.

Wilson's first speech of the tour in Columbus, Ohio, on September 4, was typical of the thirty-seven speeches he made during a journey of more than eight thousand miles over a period of twenty-three days. Wilson's appraisal of the bulk of the treaty is brief, perfunctory, almost apologetic. Most of his attention is focused upon the League itself, defining it, explaining it, even pleading for it:

. . . This treaty was not intended merely to end this war. It was intended to prevent any similar war. I wonder if some of the opponents of the League of Nations have forgotten the promises we made our people. . . . We had taken by processes of law the flower of our youth . . . if we do not end it, if we do not do the best that human concert of action can do to end it, we are of all men the most unfaithful . . . to the loving hearts who suffered in this war, the most unfaithful to those households bowed in grief and yet lifted with the feeling that the lad laid down his life for a great thing . . . in order that other lads might never have to do the same thing. That is what the League of Nations is for, to end this war justly, and then not merely to serve notice on governments which would contemplate the same things that Germany contemplated that they will do it at their peril, but also . . . to prove to them that they will do it at their peril. It is idle to say the world *will* combine against you, because it may not, but it is persuasive to say that the world *is* combined against you, and will remain combined against the things Germany attempted. The League of Nations is the only thing that can prevent the recurrence of this dreadful catastrophe and redeem our promises. (Baker-Dodd III, I, 593)

Not only was Wilson refusing to compromise with evil, as has often been pointed out by his critics, but perhaps more importantly he was unwilling to compromise the promise that he made when he took the American people into the war. And, as he makes clear, concessions or limitations, whether mild or strong, were threats not only to the promise but to the means by which it might be redeemed for the future.

Wilson's reception was good, the crowds, particularly on the West Coast, were reminiscent in size and enthusiasm of those in Europe, and Wilson's confidence grew. But at the same time his energies diminished, headaches increased, and he had trouble breathing. On September 25 he spoke at Pueblo, Colorado. That night he could not sleep, and the next morning his condition was serious. Joseph Tumulty insisted that the tour be canceled. The train returned to Washington, Wilson's last furious personal fight at an end.

For nearly two weeks the President's condition deteriorated, obviously the result of a cerebral thrombosis, but then it stabilized, his condition remaining serious, with partial paralysis, all of it concealed not only from his enemies but from the nation. By the end of October he received visitors. On November 19 the Senate rejected the treaty with the League of Nations appended. During December, pressures for compromise and acceptance increased, including efforts by former President William Howard Taft, humanitarian Herbert Hoover, and elder statesman William Jennings Bryan. But

Wilson stood firm, looking forward to the election of 1920 as a referendum on the League. His strength slowly increased, and at the same time he placed his faith in the people; perhaps he waited for a nominating call in 1920 that never came.

Pointing out the loss of his fight, the unwillingness to compromise, the near-incapacity to govern, the deterioration of personal relations, especially with Tumulty, that had sustained Wilson throughout his political career, numerous critics have suggested that perhaps it would have been better for the President and the nation had his stroke been fatal, had other men carried on the fight, perhaps compromising it into less than a victory. But Wilson lived, enjoying comparatively minor triumphs—the passage of the Nineteenth Amendment on August 26, 1919; the awarding of the Nobel Peace Prize on December 10.

On November 2, however, his League was repudiated by his people as Warren G. Harding was elected overwhelmingly to the Presidency. On March 4, 1921, he rode with Harding to the Capitol and then, with his wife, went into retirement on "S" Street in Washington, emerging only briefly and rarely, to ride in the funeral parade of the Unknown Soldier on November 11, 1921, to attend the theater on rare occasions, and to appear at the funeral of his successor on August 8, 1923. Yet he was not entirely silent; on November 10, 1923, he made a brief radio address commemorating Armistice Day and pleading once more for his League; in August he published a brief essay in the *Atlantic Monthly*, once more pleading for justice and law among men.

On Armistice Day, November 11, 1923, a group of supporters gathered before his house. In his last public appearance, he spoke briefly from the front steps, and then, after the applause had diminished, he spoke forcefully:

Just one more word. I cannot refrain from saying it. I am not one of those who has the least anxiety about the triumph of the principles I have stood for. I have seen fools resist Providence before, and I have seen their destruction. . . . That we shall prevail is as sure as that God reigns. Thank you.[2]

Wilson's courage and faith never failed, and during those last years he remained a symbol of courage and hope, particularly to those faithful who gathered before his door each Armistice Day. On January 31, 1924, as his health deteriorated seriously, that few began to gather once more, and on February 6, they were there, some kneeling, some weeping, as the President died. He is buried in the city of his triumph and failure, in the crypt of the Washington Cathedral.

CHAPTER 10

The Legacy of Wilson's Presidency

THE eight years of Woodrow Wilson's Presidency are the central fact of his existence, and every other aspect of his life is diminished accordingly, except as it relates to his tenure in the White House. Consequently, assessments of that fact began even before he rode to the Capitol with Warren G. Harding on March 4, 1921; they continue today; and they will be part of the writing of history and biography as long as the elusive meanings of his time and ours are pursued in the search for truth. No work dealing with Wilson can overlook the fact of his Presidency, and none, even a study of him as a writer, can avoid attempting an assessment.

That assessment began in the partisan political warfare of 1920. In his admittedly biased mock-heroic Socratic dialogue, *The Passing of the New Freedom,* published nearly four years before Wilson's death, James M. Beck wrote truer than he knew when he said that "Woodrow Wilson now belongs to history. His complex personality and his world-wide policies will be the subject of acute discussion for generations to come. To tell the truth about them, as one sees the truth—and who now sees it, except as through a glass darkly?—is the highest duty of citizenship. . . ."[1] In the more than half century between Beck's book and this, one still sees, perhaps always will see, Wilson as through a glass, less darkly, perhaps, now than in the heat of partisan politics and with the advantages of perspective, of experience, and the tools of modern scholarly research.

Certainly the years of his Presidency have come into clearer focus now than ever before, just as we are coming to a keener understanding of the origins and nature of the war that indelibly marked his leadership of the nation and which, in the final analysis, if one ever becomes possible, will determine the truth of the years between March 4, 1913, and March 4, 1921. Nevertheless, history is not only made up of facts; it is also made up of opinion, of what John A. Garraty describes as "what people who know what happened think about past

144

events,"[2] which, when advanced by competent historians, becomes "what are called interpretations—complex attempts to order many facts in such a way as to form consistent and thus persuasive explanations of some segment of the past."[3] As we move into the last decades of the twentieth century, we are convinced that we know most of the facts of Wilson's Presidential years, and with the advantage of our perspective we can approach validity if not truth in our assessment of the meaning and significance of those years.

The first judgment imposed on the Wilson Presidency was not historical but contemporary and political: the election of 1920; but Wilson was a historian, and he knew that the verdict of the electorate in choosing Mr. Harding and normalcy was a temporary lapse; at one time he had commented that "as compared with the verdict of the next twenty-five years, I do not care a peppercorn about the verdict of 1916," and he might have said the same in 1920. Wilson's observation in 1916 seems uncannily accurate, however, when one considers the fact that 1941 marked the entry of the United States into the Second World War, the war that Wilson had predicted and that was to be the single major fact in our contemporary assessment of his Presidency.

While Wilson himself regarded his failure in the Senate and in the election of 1920 as temporary setbacks that would lead to an ultimate vindication and acceptance of his ideas, his contemporaries and many of those who attempted to assess his Presidency in the years between the wars were skeptical of its value and doubtful of its meaning, just as they questioned or condemned American participation in the war itself. Shaped by the conviction that the Peace Conference had betrayed American sacrifices in the war, convictions that Wilson had made that betrayal possible grew stronger, until at times his critics blamed him for American participation in an unnecessary and vicious war for commercial supremacy. Marxist and economic historians, buoyed by the findings in the mid-1930s of the so-called Nye Committee of the Senate, under the chairmanship of Gerald Nye of North Dakota, supported the charge that America's participation in the war had been the result of Wilson's ineptness or worse. The committee's revelations were sensational and scandalous as they documented or purported to document a war fought for profits—the extremely high profits of industrialists and munitions makers—and further suggested that Wilson would not have taken the nation to war had the economic stakes not been so great.

The practical political results of the Nye Committee were the Neutrality Acts of 1935–1939, a series of laws that denied Wilson his justification for American entry into the war as they sought to make a future repetition impossible. As Hitler's troops marched into the Rhineland and prepared for later, greater excursions, as Italian aggression in Ethiopia and Japanese aggression in China went unchecked, and as civil war intensified in Spain, the acts prohibited American loans or credits to belligerents, placed embargoes on shipments of munitions, and, in the ultimate denial of Wilson's insistence upon the rights of neutrals, forbade Americans to travel on belligerents' ships and to arm American merchantmen. Concurrently, the Senate once more rejected American membership in the World Court, as the acts seemed to be a final triumph for William Jennings Bryan's insistence upon a retreat from war and a posthumous denial of Wilson's insistence upon the preservation of traditional American rights. Wilson's stock had never been lower in the popular or scholarly American mind as it seemed that American participation in the war, the greatest fact of Wilson's Presidency, had been a tragic, avoidable mistake.

With the outbreak of another major European war in the fall of 1939 while the first strong, progressive President since Wilson occupied the White House, a President who had already built substantial economic reforms upon the foundation of Wilson's domestic program, American policy and legislation began to change, and with those changes, Wilson's failure or his ineptness began increasingly to be seen as a tragic prophetic vision. The series of great events of the Roosevelt years, beginning with the "cash and carry" support for the Allied cause and its natural successor, "Lend-Lease," carrying through the attack on Pearl Harbor and ultimately, after Roosevelt's death, culminating in victory in Europe and the Pacific and the San Francisco Conference of the United Nations, provided Roosevelt's vindication and Wilson's at the same time.

The years since the end of the Second World War have seen the rehabilitation of Wilson's reputation and the growth of a massive Wilson scholarship and a major Presidential reinterpretation. Wilson is still seen as a tragic figure—he will always be that—but he is seen, too, as a man of great accomplishment as well as of great failure, a great President in spite of as well as because of his great failure.

As a war President, Wilson has found his place in the first rank with Abraham Lincoln and Franklin Delano Roosevelt. Like them, he did not make war hastily or foolishly. Those critics who insisted that he had gone to war too late are long dead, and those who criticize him for going at all are virtually silent. As did Lincoln before him and

Roosevelt a generation later, he took a badly prepared nation to war, built the finest fighting machine of his time, and won the greatest victory of his age. That alone is a substantial accomplishment.

But, like Lincoln and Roosevelt, Wilson's war leadership was much greater than the victory alone suggests. Wilson's war Presidency, like theirs, was concerned with the meaning and the ends of the war, and even as he sought the victory he continued to articulate the reasons for the war and its goals.

In so doing he defined the meaning of the war for the nation and the world many times. In his message to the joint session of Congress on April 2, 1917, he not only requested a declaration of war against the Imperial German Government, but he explained the reasons for that request and then went beyond definition to envision its ends, in the process inadvertently giving the war the simplistic slogan that explained it to the popular mind. But Wilson went even further in his effort to shape the peace that would follow victory. The renunciation of conquest, of indemnities, of spoils and compensation was without precedent, and he added to those renunciations his positive goals: the right of small nations to liberty; the right of people everywhere to a voice in their government; a world free from war in the future, thereby coining another popular slogan.

But Wilson's attempt to define the meaning and the ends of the war did not rest with the coining of popular slogans; on Flag Day, June 14, 1917, he declared the war a "People's War"—a war for the liberation and safety of all peoples, the German included. With his faith in language and reason and in the innate wisdom of the people, on January 18, 1918, he once more articulated, in greater detail, the purpose and meaning of the peace as he spoke again to a joint session of Congress. In doing so, in what became known as his "Fourteen Points," he made that purpose and meaning clear not only to Americans but to people over much of the world. Like Lincoln's Emancipation Proclamation, Wilson's Fourteen Points were a great war document and a great peace document, and the words have never been denied.

Self-styled realists pointed out for two decades that those points were idealistic and impractical, that the facts of the events at the Peace Conference and in the United States Senate proved their impracticality, that Wilson the idealist had not only been outmaneuvered at the Paris Peace Conference but had been taught the facts of political life at home. But these assertions, we know now, tell only part of the truth. We know that Wilson had not "lost" at Paris, that he had "won" the most important concession: the creation of the League of Nations, the instrument that would right the wrongs perpetuated by the Versailles Treaty, that would ultimately teach us to make peace, and that would then bring order and reason to a world still chaotic and irrational. Rather than a defeat for Wilson's idealism, it was a victory for his sense of reality, for what Arthur S. Link has called his "higher realism."[4] The failure of Versailles was not Wilson's failure, nor had the failure been the result of European conspiracies; it was an American failure, as we learned on that morning when Japanese bombers appeared over Battleship Row in Pearl Harbor.

Wilson's failure in his attempt to secure American ratification of the Treaty with its League of Nations unfettered was no more a conflict between realism and idealism than was the Peace Conference, nor was his refusal to compromise, to save the League at the cost of reservations, the stubborn querulousness of a sick, frustrated old man. We know that he should have compromised, but that he did not, and we know, from posthumous diagnosis—admittedly a dangerous practice, even in the light of great advances in the diagnostician's art—that he did suffer a stroke in Pueblo, as he apparently had in Paris, that it was severe, and that his subsequent behavior was typical of stroke victims as it resulted in strained loyalties, broken friendships of long standing, and a dogmatic refusal to yield to the illness or to well-meaning, sensible advice. Wilson's failure was not of his vision or his will; more than anything else, it was a physical betrayal that he could neither foresee, nor, even with the support of his wife and his physician, overcome and control.

On balance, with the perspective of three later wars and a struggle for the ideological leadership of the world, with an imperfect United Nations and a permanent peace not yet on the horizon, with a greater but still imperfect wisdom in the ways of men and nations, we recognize the immensity of Wilson's vision and the practicality of his attempt to make it real. Not Wilson but his contemporaries, European as well as American, were shortsighted and naive in Paris and Washington. We approach Wilson with a greater understanding and a more profound sympathy, and we see him as the great President in war and in the search for peace that he was.

In considering the drama as well as the magnitude of Wilson's leadership in making war and seeking peace, too frequently in the past we have overlooked or understressed his accomplishments in reordering the political, social, and economic order of the nation, and again the result has been an incomplete and unfair assessment of his

Presidency. But perspective again permits us to see clearer and more distantly, and the sheer accomplishment of his dedication to his "New Freedom," his articulation of purpose, and his skillful leadership is impressive: currency and tariff reform, passage of the Clayton Anti-Trust Act, establishment of the Federal Trade Commission and the Federal Reserve system. Whether or not he became increasingly supportive of government intervention and activism in 1916 is irrelevant to his accomplishment as a result: federal rural credits, a child-labor bill, a federal inheritance tax and an increased income tax, the eight-hour day for interstate railroaders. No less irrelevant is the judgment, misguided but sincere, that he had permitted progressivism to become a casualty of war, a view that ignores his insistence while the war came to its climax that women's suffrage become constitutional reality.

Wilson's accomplishment was substantial in itself, but it had two important results that we no longer overlook. He revitalized the office of the Presidency, a fact that was unnoticed until normalcy and its failure had run their course; and he laid the philosophic and legislative foundations for the social and economic reforms that followed the restoration of Presidential authority in 1933.

The product of his long observation of the workings of government, his experience as president of Princeton, and his reform successes as Governor of New Jersey, Wilson's concept of the Presidency was clear and complex: the President was not only the nation's Chief Executive, but he was leader of his political party, formulator and innovator in legislative matters as well as the ultimate executor of law, and national spokesman in everything, particularly in foreign policy and international relations. Wilson had come into office determined to put this concept of the Presidency into practice, determined, too, to be President in fact and to insure that his judgment would prevail. These principles had transformed Princeton from an obscure, genteel college into a major university, and they had permitted him to capture control of New Jersey from the political bosses and make the state a model of progressive reform. He had no doubt of their effectiveness in the Presidency and the nation as well.

Some scholars have ascribed Wilson's concept of the Presidency to his admiration for the British legislative system and the office of the prime ministership, and in a sense this is true, particularly in his determination to be the leader of his party in Congress. This admiration may have been the rationale behind a major innovation that Presidents who succeeded him have followed to their advantage and ignored to their peril: his presentation of major policies and messages to the Congress in person. But he went beyond any concept of a prime ministership in another major innovation that has permanently changed the office of the President: his use of the full powers of the office in molding public opinion, an important force in controlling his party and directing the legislative process to insure the success of his programs.

Not only have Wilson's innovations in the exercise of Presidential power become part of the public expectation of the President in office, but to a great extent succeeding Presidents have been measured in terms of the Wilson example. Furthermore, a number of Presidents, particularly Franklin Roosevelt, Harry S. Truman, John Kennedy, and Lyndon Johnson, have consciously tried to emulate him. His portrait occupied a prominent place on the Oval Office wall during the Presidency of Richard Nixon, suggesting, perhaps, the origin if not etymology of a practice and a verb known as "stonewalling."

Wilson's concept of the Presidency was not only crucial in securing the passage of his domestic reform program, but it provided the foundation of the theory and practice of the reform Presidents of the next generation. Roosevelt's "Hundred Days" that followed his inauguration were, in effect, extensions of the Wilson Presidency, intensified and refined by economic crisis. Furthermore, in the international dimension the United Nations was the creation of Wilson as much as of Franklin Roosevelt.

Wilson's domestic successes, like Roosevelt's, were perhaps made possible by circumstances—the dominance of the progressive impulse in 1913 anticipating the demands of the depression in 1933, the Democratic majorities that each enjoyed in Congress, the determination of the Democratic party in both cases to perform spectacularly and well after long periods of Republican dominance. But in neither case would the potential for change have become real had the President not used the full powers of his office creatively as well as politically. Conversely, the tragedy of Herbert Hoover is that, having known and admired Wilson, he did not emulate him. Only later, a generation after his own Presidency, could Hoover write, with sympathy and understanding, his interpretation of Wilson and his Presidency in *The Ordeal of Woodrow Wilson.*

Wilson's ordeal in the Presidency, to use Hoover's term, provides the substance of his legacy to the American system of government, to the responsibility of government to the individual citizen, and the responsibility of the American nation to the world of which it is a part. His legacy is a political philosophy, a pattern of action, and, to a great extent, a way of life, all of which combine to form the basis of his place in the hierarchy of American Presidents. Certainly Wilson is and will remain in the first rank of those who held that office; he may be one of the first five, with Thomas Jefferson, Andrew Jackson, Abraham Lincoln, and Franklin Delano Roosevelt.

But a reputation is not a true legacy unless it is understood. This legacy is found in the course of action, the political philosophy, the fusion of realism and idealism and of success and failure that he passed on to his successors. As we grow in understanding, we know, too, that his legacy is also in the creative documents that he left behind, the result of his faith in language and reason as the raw materials of truth. Not inconsequential is his legacy as a man of letters.

CHAPTER 11

Woodrow Wilson, Man of Letters

IN the half century since Wilson's passing, many attempts have been made to assess the meaning of his life and death, but a final judgment is yet to come. Perhaps none can be made; perhaps none ever will. Like many of his great predecessors and followers in the Presidency, Wilson was greater than the sum of his parts—the qualities that made him what he was and that made his Presidency what it was. Perhaps only one thing can be said with certainty about Wilson, just as it is the only thing that can be said with certainty about his predecessor Abraham Lincoln and his successor Franklin Delano Roosevelt: he was a great man.

The essence of that greatness is elusive because it is visionary rather than real, although many of its dimensions are real enough: his concept of the moral dimensions of leadership; his definitions of human progress; his insistence upon the practical perfectibility of human institutions; his recognition that there were causes greater than himself, his Presidency, or his life. Perhaps more than anything else, the tangible measure of his greatness is the degree to which he extended the domain of human freedom in domestic political warfare as well as in the horror of the greatest war man had yet known. Neither war, Wilson insisted, was too great a price to pay if only human freedom was expanded, perhaps only a little, as a result.

These tangible dimensions of his greatness have had tangible results, both positive and negative, and perhaps his failure to achieve American participation in the League of Nations is a failure that far outweighs whatever victories he may have gained. Indeed, in many respects Wilson's record of failure, both personal and public, is perhaps greater than that of his successes: perennial ill health; failure to achieve early ambitions; failure as a lawyer; political failure at Princeton; the ultimate failures at Versailles and in the Senate. But these were failures neither of the will nor of the vision, and, when all the evidence is in, it becomes evident that they were not the result of

152

failures inherent in Wilson's personality, as some critics insist; rather they were failures that resulted from the short sight of other men who were unable to share Wilson's vision either because they could not see it or, perhaps more properly, because they would not see it. If Wilson's unwillingness or inability to compromise with wrong is a major source of the failures that dominated his life, if his moralistic nature demanded too much of himself and others, if his mission and that of his God sometimes became confused—and his critics are certainly justified in pointing out these and other shortcomings in personality—nevertheless his causes—whether they were academic or political, domestic or international, based in the search for victory in war or peace in victory—have been justified by the course of history in the more than fifty years since his death. And the causes of his enemies have been revealed by history as irresponsible if not vicious, inept if not evil.

But in the final analysis, failure is not greatness, although many great men have failed; indeed, perhaps the ultimate test of greatness is, as William Faulkner insisted, not the measure of accomplishment, the list of successes great and small, or the approval of critics or historians; the test of greatness as Faulkner defined it is the magnificence of the vision, of the attempt to expand the dimensions of the human spirit, and of the inevitable failure that becomes itself magnificent.

To Faulkner's definition, however, must be added the dimensions of the attempt to communicate that vision, of a faith in the human ability to speak, to listen, and to understand. Wilson believed firmly in the perfectibility, under God, of man and his institutions, a faith that combined the heritage of Calvinists, Rationalists, and Romantics, all of whose attitudes combined to produce American tradition and Wilson's idealism. His Calvinism is apparent in his view of the human mission as a reflection of God's will and in a conviction that the traditional human institutions, particularly religious and educational, are the means by which that mission may be carried out; like the Rationalists he trusted man's mind and particularly the ability of the human mind to perceive order and perfection in the mind and works of God and emulate them in his own affairs; like the Romantics, he believed in the innate goodness, worth, and perfectibility of mankind. All his life he sought to translate these articles of faith into workable human institutions and patterns of behavior.

This faith is the essence of his greatness, and its perception had been made possible by the greatest of his roles, that which he practiced throughout his life. More than anything else, Wilson was a teacher, committed to the written and spoken word as, in the Emersonian sense, one mind might communicate with others on increasingly complex levels through increasingly complex symbols until the two become metaphorically and spiritually one. Wilson's abiding faith, then, after his faith in God, was in language, and he carried on in the tradition of that faith to the end of his life and, in the thousands of documents, ranging from books and essays to speeches, memos, and letters, beyond his life and as far on into the future as one can foresee.

Wilson was neither a great writer nor a great man of letters, and although he has been called both and has also been called a failure at writing, there is no real evidence to support conjecture about his ambition to be either. Although Wilson was aware of the aesthetic and intellectual qualities of language, he never regarded them as ends of writing, but as means by which he might more effectively reach his ends.

For Wilson, language, whether written or spoken, was a means to the end that he sought: to communicate that which he saw within himself, whether it be the nature of man's institutions, the pattern of his behavior, or, increasingly, in terms at once visionary and practical, the means by which both might be improved, might, indeed, even approach perfection.

In practical critical terms Wilson was a good but not great writer; he was a better but not yet great speaker. Contrary to the attempt by William Bayard Hale to destroy Wilson's reputation as a writer in his *The Story of a Style*, Wilson's writing ability, like the path of his thought, cannot be destroyed because it is to a great extent the means by which the essence of his greatness, the nature of his vision, was defined for his time and for the duration of man's continued concern with the search for justice, mercy, and peace. Nowhere else has man's right to determine and control his own destiny been articulated more clearly or completely, nor has anyone defined it with more consistent eloquence, as the untutored, unsophisticated peoples of much of the earth heard it and understood it. That Wilson's vision has yet to become real is not a mark of failure, his numerous critics notwithstanding, as Faulkner made clear; indeed, the harshness of many of those critics is perhaps further proof of his greatness.

Perhaps the greatest lesson Wilson taught, the subject of his writing and speaking from his undergraduate days at Princeton to the house on "S" Street in his retirement, was the closeness of the relationship between man and his institutions, that not only were they inseparable in this world, but that through them men expressed themselves, whether they knew it or not, and controlled their own destiny at the same time. Thus, ultimately, they controlled the forces of the future, and, by the extent to which they applied their God-given intelligence to their own institutions, they determined, for better or worse, their own fate and that of generations unborn.

Such a conviction is not insignificant, but in the context of Wilson's time and our own, it is denied by men with little faith or hope, destroyed by those who lack charity, distorted by those who seek power for their own ends, denigrated by those who reduce or deny the significance of the individual. Yet, as Wilson believed, man was God's greatest creation; the state, for better or worse, was man's. In his attempt to persuade men that they could contribute to man's progress he was at once and in numerous instances eloquent, compelling, clear, and persuasive. In practical terms many of his works remain classics of their sort; in the visionary terms in which man's ideals are phrased, his work is both classic and timely, and it will remain so until his prediction, "That we shall prevail is as sure as that God reigns," is fulfilled.

Notes and References

Chapter One

1. For the biographical and genealogical facts of Wilson's life and background, I am indebted to Ray Stannard Baker, *Woodrow Wilson, Life and Letters,* 8 vols. (Garden City, 1927–1939); John C. Garraty, *Woodrow Wilson* (New York, 1956); and the major study by Arthur S. Link, *Woodrow Wilson: The Road to the White House* (Princeton, 1947); *The New Freedom* (Princeton, 1956); *The Struggle for Neutrality, 1914–1915* (Princeton, 1960); *Campaigns for Progressivism and Peace, 1916–1917* (Princeton, 1965).

2. Ray Stannard Baker, *Woodrow Wilson, Life and Letters:* Vol. I: *Youth,* Garden City, 1927; p. 22. Henceforth all references to this work will appear after appropriate quotations by "Baker," followed by volume and page numbers.

3. Quoted in Ira Mothner, *Woodrow Wilson: Champion of Peace*, New York, 1969, p. 17.

4. Woodrow Wilson, "Cabinet Government in the United States," in *The Public Papers of Woodrow Wilson,* Vol. I, "College and State" edited by Ray Stannard Baker and William E. Dodd (New York, 1925), p. 19. Future references to this source will include "Baker-Dodd," the appropriate volume number and page number after the appropriate quotation.

Chapter Two

1. Mothner, p. 22.

2. John M. Blum, *Woodrow Wilson and the Politics of Morality* (Boston, 1956), p. 16, and Sigmund Freud and William C. Bullitt, *Thomas Woodrow Wilson: A Psychological Study* (Boston, 1966), pp. 94–95.

Chapter Three

1. Woodrow Wilson, *Congressional Government: A Study in American Politics* (New York, 1956), p. 28.

2. *Ibid.,* p. 56.

3. *Ibid.*

4. *Ibid.,* pp. 58–59.

5. *Ibid.,* p. 103.

6. *Ibid.*, p. 141.

7. *Ibid.*, p. 144.

8. *Ibid.*, p. 171.

9. *Ibid.*, p. 173.

10. *Ibid.*, pp. 191–92.

11. *Ibid.*, p. 215.

12. *Ibid.*

13. *Ibid.*, p. 205.

14. Walter Lippmann, Introduction to *Congressional Government: A Study in American Politics,* pp. 13–14.

15. *Ibid.*, p. 8.

Chapter Four

1. Woodrow Wilson, "Of the Study of Politics" reprinted in Woodrow Wilson, *Selected Literary and Political Papers,* Vol. I, New York, 1921, p. 49.

2. Walter Lippmann, Introduction to *Congressional Government*, p. 13.

3. Woodrow Wilson, *The State: Elements of Historical and Practical Politics* (Boston, 1911), p. 628.

4. *Ibid.*, pp. 656–57.

5. *Ibid.*, pp. 659–61.

6. *Ibid.*

7. *Ibid.*

Chapter Five

1. Woodrow Wilson, "University Training and Citizenship," the *Forum*, August 23, 1894, reprinted in Baker-Dodd I, p. 228.

2. *Ibid.*, p. 258.

3. Woodrow Wilson, *Division and Reunion, 1829–1889* (New York, 1893), p. viii.

4. *Ibid.*, p. 292.

5. *Ibid.*

6. *Ibid.*, p. 299.

7. *Ibid.*

8. Woodrow Wilson, *The Papers of Woodrow Wilson*, edited by Arthur S. Link *et al.*, Vol. VIII (Princeton, 1970), p. 220. Hereafter references to this series will appear after the appropriate quotation as "Papers," followed by volume and page numbers.

9. Woodrow Wilson, *An Old Master and Other Political Essays* (New York, 1893), reprinted in Wilson, *Selected Literary and Political Papers and Addresses*, Vol. III, p. 9.

10. *Ibid.*, pp. 9–10.

11. *Ibid.*, p. 17.

12. *Ibid.*, p. 22.

13. *Ibid.*

14. *Ibid.*, pp. 22–23.

15. *Ibid.*, pp. 23–24.

16. *Ibid.*, p. 48.

17. *Ibid.*, p. 115.

18. See editors' note, Papers VIII, pp. 238–40.

19. Woodrow Wilson, *Mere Literature and Other Essays* (Boston, 1896), pp. 1–2.

20. *Ibid.*, p. 3.

21. *Ibid.*, p. 8.

22. *Ibid.*, p. 9.

23. *Ibid.*, pp. 13–14.

24. *Ibid.*, p. 26.

25. *Ibid.*, p. 53.

26. *Ibid.*, p. 61.

27. *Ibid.*, pp. 99–100.

28. *Ibid.*, p. 159.

29. *Ibid.*, p. 185.

30. *Ibid.*, p. 187.

31. *Ibid.*, p. 189.

32. *Ibid.*, p. 191.

33. *Ibid.*, p. 197.

34. *Ibid.*, p. 201.

35. *Ibid.*

36. *Ibid.*, p. 211.

37. *Ibid.*, p. 212.

38. *Ibid.*, p. 26.

39. Woodrow Wilson, *George Washington* (New York, 1893), pp. 3–4.

40. *Ibid.*, p. 66.

41. *Ibid.*, p. 77.

42. *Ibid.*, p. 288.

43. *Ibid.*, pp. 296–97.

44. *Ibid.*, p. 313.

45. Woodrow Wilson, *When a Man Comes to Himself* (New York, 1901), reprinted in *Selected Literary and Political Papers and Addresses III,* p. 17.

Chapter Six

1. Woodrow Wilson, *A History of the American People* (New York, 1902), Vol. V, p. 300.

2. *Ibid.*, p. 299.

3. Woodrow Wilson, *Constitutional Government in the United States,* New York, 1908, pp. 64–65.

4. *Ibid.*, p. 222.

Chapter Seven

1. Josephus Daniels, *Life of Woodrow Wilson*, N.P., 1924, p. 99.
2. *Ibid.*

Chapter Eight

1. Theodore Roosevelt, *Collected Works,* Vol. XVII (New York, 1927), p. 254.
2. Woodrow Wilson, *The New Freedom* (New York, 1913), p. 18.
3. *Ibid.*
4. *Ibid.*, p. 35.
5. Woodrow Wilson, *Crossroads of Freedom,* edited by John Wells Davidson (New York, 1956), p. 245.
6. *The New Freedom*, p. 19.
7. *Ibid.*, p. 21.
8. *Ibid.*, pp. 22–23.
9. *Ibid.*, p. 32.
10. *Ibid.*, p. 37.
11. *Ibid.*, p.42.
12. *Ibid.*, p. 77.
13. *Ibid.*, pp. 64–65.
14. *Ibid.*, p. 105.
15. See, for example, Herbert Croly's remarks in the *New Republic*, I (November 21, 1914), p. 7.

Chapter Nine

1. Blum, *Woodrow Wilson and the Politics of Morality,* pp. 117–18.
2. John A. Garraty, *Woodrow Wilson* (New York, 1956), p. 194.

Chapter Ten

1. James M. Beck, *The Passing of the New Freedom* (New York, 1920), p. vii.
2. John A. Garraty, *Interpreting American History* (New York, 1970), p. vii.
3. *Ibid.*
4. See Link's expanded definition in "The Higher Realism of Woodrow Wilson," *Journal of Presbyterian History,* XLI (January, 1963), pp. 1-13. The essay has been frequently reprinted.

Selected Bibliography

PRIMARY SOURCES

1. The Published Writings of Woodrow Wilson

Congressional Government: A Study in American Politics. Boston: Houghton Mifflin Co., 1885.

The State: Elements of Historical and Practical Politics. Boston: D. C. Heath & Co., 1889.

Division and Reunion, 1829-1889. New York: Longmans, Green, and Co., 1893.

An Old Master and Other Political Essays. New York: Charles Scribner's Sons, 1893.

Mere Literature and Other Essays, Boston: Houghton Mifflin Co., 1896.

George Washington. New York: Harper and Brothers, 1896.

When A Man Comes to Himself. New York: Harper and Brothers, 1901.

A History of the American People. 5 vols. New York: Harper and Brothers, 1902.

Constitutional Government in the United States. New York: Columbia University Press, 1908.

The New Freedom. New York: Doubleday, Page & Company, 1913.

International Ideals: Speeches and Addresses Made During the President's European Trip. New York: Harper & Bros., 1919.

The Public Papers of Woodrow Wilson. 6 vols. in 3. Edited by Ray Stannard Baker and William E. Dodd. New York: Harper and Brothers, 1925–1927.

Selected Literary and Political papers and addresses of Woodrow Wilson. 3 vols. New York: Grosset & Dunlap, 1925–1926.

Crossroads of Freedom: the 1912 Campaign Speeches of Woodrow Wilson. Edited by John Wells Davidson with a preface by Charles Seymour. New Haven: Yale University Press, 1956.

The Political Thought of Woodrow Wilson. Edited by E. David Cronon. Indianapolis: Bobbs-Merrill Company, 1965.

The Papers of Thomas Woodrow Wilson. Edited by Arthur Stanley Link *et al.* 15 vols. to date. Princeton: Princeton University Press, 1966–.

2. Outstanding Collections of Manuscripts

The Papers of Woodrow Wilson in the Library of Congress.

The Papers of Woodrow Wilson in the Princeton University Library.

SECONDARY SOURCES

1. Books

BAKER, RAY STANNARD. *Woodrow Wilson, Life and Letters.* 8 vols. Garden City: Doubleday, Page & Co., 1927–1939. The authorized biography, a dedicated, sympathetic, and thorough but uneven work.

———. *What Wilson Did at Paris.* Garden City, N.Y.: Doubleday, Page & Co., 1920.

———. *Woodrow Wilson and World Settlement.* 3 vols. Garden City, N.Y.: Doubleday, Page & Co., 1922.

BAILEY, THOMAS A. *Woodrow Wilson and the Lost Peace.* New York: Macmillan Co., 1944. A good analysis.

———. *Woodrow Wilson and the Great Betrayal.* New York: Macmillan Co., 1945. A sequel to above. Both are close analyses.

BECK, JAMES M. *The Passing of the New Freedom.* New York: George A. Doran, 1920. An attack on Wilson's record.

BELL, HERBERT C. F. *Woodrow Wilson and the People.* Garden City, N.Y.: Doubleday, Doran and Co., 1945. A warm but somewhat apologetic work.

BLUM, JOHN MORTON. *Joe Tumulty and the Wilson Era.* Hamden, Conn.: Anchor Books, 1969. Insights into the Democratic Party as it functioned in the Wilson Era.

———. *Woodrow Wilson and the Politics of Morality.* Boston: Little, Brown and Company, 1956. A fine analysis of Wilson as a traditional moralist.

CANFIELD, LEON H. *The Presidency of Woodrow Wilson: Prelude to a World in Crisis.* Rutherford, N.J.: Farleigh Dickinson University Press, 1966. Particularly good on the early Presidency and the relationship of Wilson's Presidency to the future.

COLBY, BAINBRIDGE. *The Close of Woodrow Wilson's Administration and the Final Years.* New York: M. Kennerly, 1930. Good information on the last years by Wilson's friend.

CREEL, GEORGE. *The War, the World, and Wilson.* New York: Harper & Brothers, 1920. A defense of Wilson's war and peace policies.

Daniels, Jonathon. *The End of Innocence.* Philadelphia: Lippincott, 1954. A stimulating social history of the Wilson years.

DANIELS, JOSEPHUS. *The Life of Woodrow Wilson, 1856–1924.* N. P., 1924. An intimate and sympathetic portrayal.

———. *The Wilson Era: Years of Peace, 1910–1917.* Chapel Hill: University of North Carolina Press, 1944. The third volume of Daniels's memoirs, it gives insight into Wilson's Progressivism.

DIAMOND, WILLIAM. *The Economic Thought of Woodrow Wilson.* Baltimore:

Johns Hopkins Press, 1943. Good detail on Wilson's early economic theories.

DODD, WILLIAM E. *Woodrow Wilson and His Work.* Garden City, N. Y.: Doubleday, Page & Co., 1924. A eulogistic memoir by Ray Stannard Baker's collaborator.

FREUD, SIGMUND, and WILLIAM C. BULLITT. *Thomas Woodrow Wilson: A Psychological Study.* Boston: Houghton Mifflin Co., 1966. An attempt to demonstrate Wilson's disturbed nature that fails in fact as well as in interpretations.

GARRATY, JOHN A. *Interpreting American History.* New York: Macmillan, 1970. An interesting series of "conversations."

———. *Woodrow Wilson.* New York: Alfred A. Knopf, 1956. A good brief life.

———. *Henry Cabot Lodge: A Biography.* New York: Alfred A. Knopf, 1953. A close analysis of the depths of the conflict with Wilson.

GEORGE, ALEXANDER L. and JULIETTE L. GEORGE. *Woodrow Wilson and Colonel House.* New York: Dover Publications, 1964. An analysis of the relationship between the two.

GRAYSON, CARY T. *Woodrow Wilson: An Intimate Memoir.* New York: Holt, Rinehart and Winston, 1960. A defense of Wilson the man by his physician.

HALE, WILLIAM BAYARD. *Woodrow Wilson: The Story of His life.* Garden City, N.Y.: Doubleday, Page, 1912. A good campaign biography.

———. *The Story of a Style.* New York: B. W. Huebsch, 1920. An attack on Wilson as a writer and thinker.

HOOVER, HERBERT. *The Ordeal of Woodrow Wilson.* New York: McGraw Hill Book Co., 1950. A sympathetic analysis of Wilson's role in the Presidency during the war and after.

HOUSE, EDWARD M. *The Intimate Papers of Colonel House.* Ed. by Charles Seymour. 4 vols. Boston: Houghton Mifflin Co., 1926–1928. Neither a biography nor an edition of papers but something of both, it makes clear the House role.

JOHNSON, GERALD W. *Woodrow Wilson.* New York: Harper & Brothers, 1944. A fine photographic collection.

KERNEY, JAMES. *The Political Education of Woodrow Wilson.* New York: The Century Co., 1926. A good character analysis, emphasizing Wilson's governorship.

LAWRENCE, DAVID. *The True Story of Woodrow Wilson.* New York: George H. Doran Co., 1924. A fair, stimulating study, based upon personal knowledge.

LANSING, ROBERT. *The Peace Negotiations: A Personal Narrative.* Boston: Houghton Mifflin Co., 1921. An insider's view, including his break with Wilson.

———. *The Big Four.* Boston: Houghton Mifflin Co., 1921. Candid views of the negotiators.

LINK, ARTHUR S. *Wilson the Diplomatist: A Look at His Major Foreign Policies.* Baltimore: Johns Hopkins Press, 1957. A study of the evolution from neutrality through belligerancy to peace.

———. *Woodrow Wilson and the Progressive Era.* New York: Harper & Bros., 1954. A study of Wilson's domestic policies and attitudes.

———. *Wilson: The Road to the White House.* Princeton: Princeton University Press, 1947. The first volume of Link's definitive biography.

———. *Wilson: The New Freedom.* Princeton: Princeton University Press, 1956. The second volume, emphasizing the early Presidency.

———. *Wilson: The Struggle for Neutrality, 1914–1915.* Princeton: Princeton University Press, 1960. The third volume.

———. *Wilson: Campaigns for Progressivism and Peace, 1916–1917.* Princeton: Princeton University Press, 1965. The fourth volume.

———. *Woodrow Wilson: A Brief Biography.* Cleveland: World Publishing Co., 1963. One of the best short biographies.

LOTH, DAVID. *Woodrow Wilson: The Fifteenth Point.* Philadelphia: Lippincott, 1941. A generally sympathetic interpretation of Wilson's personality.

LOW, A. MAURICE. *Woodrow Wilson: An Interpretation.* Boston: Little, Brown and Co., 1919. A sympathetic contemporary interpretation.

McADOO, WILLIAM GIBBS. *Crowded Years.* New York: Houghton Mifflin Co., 1931. A general memoir by Wilson's son-in-law.

MOTHNER, IRA. *Woodrow Wilson: Champion of Peace.* New York: Franklin Watts, Inc., 1969. A brief but interesting, friendly appraisal of Wilson's search for world peace.

TUMULTY, JOSEPH P. *Woodrow Wilson As I Know Him.* Garden City: Doubleday Page & Co., 1921. A memoir that is not reliable, by Wilson's secretary.

WILSON, EDITH B. *My Memoir.* Indianapolis: Bobbs-Merrill Co., 1938. Revealing personal recollections, especially of the period of Wilson's incapacity.

2. Essays

LINK, ARTHUR S. "The Higher Realism of Woodrow Wilson." *Journal of Presbyterian History,* XLI (January 1963), 1–13. Insight into Wilson's concept of duty and responsibility in a seminal essay.

LIPPMANN, WALTER. Introduction to W. W., *Congressional Government: A Study in American Politics.* New York: Meridian Books, 1956. An interesting interpretive essay.

Index

(References to Wilson's works will be found under the author's name.)

164